HORSESHOES

HORSESHOES

Steven Boga

STACKPOLE
BOOKS

Published by
STACKPOLE BOOKS
5067 Ritter Road
Mechanicsburg, PA 17055

Printed in the United States of America

10 9 8 7 6 5 4 3 2 1

First edition

Cover design by Caroline Miller with Wendy Baugher

Library of Congress Cataloging-in-Publication Data

Boga, Steve, 1947–
    Horseshoes / Steven Boga.—1st ed.
        p. cm.
    ISBN 0-8117-2490-5 (pbk.)
    1. Horseshoe pitching.   I. Title.
  GV1095.B65   1996
  796.24—dc20   96–23096
                                                        CIP

CONTENTS

....

Introduction vi

History of Horseshoes 1

Court and Equipment 6

Grip, Stance, and Swing 15

Strategy 29

Winning the Mental Game 33

Getting Better 39

Rules 57

Glossary 75

Resources 78

INTRODUCTION

· ·

*Horseshoes is a very good thing to do
when you have no need or desire to
pretend to be heroic.*
                                        —Sports Illustrated

I confess that I find excellence highly compelling. I have interviewed dozens of athletic champions, mostly in unsung adventure sports, and found that it doesn't matter whether the sport is popular or obscure, life threatening or just tendon twanging. The few who excel merit our attention for their marvelous accomplishments—regardless of profitability or risk level.

There's certainly nothing very risky about pitching horseshoes, but there is something refreshingly basic and straightforward about it. Consider its origin: Greek and Roman foot soldiers, following in the hoofsteps of their armies' horses, picked up discarded shoes and tossed them at a target. Simple, earthy.

There are other pluses: Horseshoes can be played alone or with other people, anywhere by almost anyone; it is portable and inexpensive; it is challenging enough to be satisfying when you pitch well; it is surprisingly good exercise.

Although pitching horseshoes is a simple sport, it is not easy to master. Let's say that you're a talented beginner. You are athletic, have a good arm, and can fling a dense slab of metal 40 feet and hit a dime. You'll still need a lot of luck to nail ringers one out of ten tries.

On the other hand, great pitchers average seven or eight ringers per ten throws, and one of the best pitchers in the world, Walter Ray Williams, Jr., regularly nails nine out of ten ringers and has thrown perfect games.

But even if your ringer average hovers around zero, you can have heaps of fun with horseshoes. Several million people do it with some regularity in their backyards, at picnics, behind firehouses and gas stations, in churchyards and prison yards, at summer camp and in retirement communities, and just about anywhere you can pound a couple of pieces of pipe into the ground and throw horseshoes at 'em—even the White House lawn. It's a touch of Americana that harks back to the halcyon days of small towns and Norman Rockwell intimacy. Our great-grandparents played the game, and so will our great-grandchildren.

To maximize your horseshoe fun, find your level of competition, strive to improve, and don't ever play Walter Ray for money.

It's been said that horseshoes, golf, and bowling, three popular accuracy games, are all about equally as difficult to master. That is, regularly throwing 70 percent or 80 percent ringers is comparable to playing par golf or carrying a 200 bowling average.

Although the complete laws of horseshoe pitching appear in the rules chapter, you should have at least a rudimentary understanding of the game before you tackle technique and strategy. Most people understand the basics: Throw a set of shoes from one end to the other, walk to them, bend over and pick them up, throw the other way.

Here's a bit more detail, using cancellation scoring.

In singles, one player throws two shoes at the stake at the opposite end. Then the other player throws two shoes at the same stake. That's an inning. Now you both walk to the other end, figure the score, pick up the shoes, and throw them back again. This continues until either you throw an agreed-upon number of shoes or one of you reaches an agreed-upon score.

You get three points for a ringer, one point for closest (within 6 inches of the stake), nothing for leaners. Ties cancel out—that is, your ringer zeroes out my ringer. But if you throw two ringers to my one, you get three points for the unmatched ringer. If we both throw one shoe that lands within 6 inches of the stake, only the closest shoe scores a point. If your two shoes are both within 6 inches of the stake and closer to it than either of my shoes, you score two points. At no time do both players score in the same inning. The player who scores goes first the next inning; if neither player scores, the lead alternates.

The following throws do not score (although these rules are often ignored in backyard play):

1. Any shoe thrown by a player who steps over the foul line.
2. Any shoe that bounces out of the pit area or hits a backboard, regardless of where it eventually comes to rest.

• • • • • •

Besides the usual thanks to the people who read manuscripts before they become books, especially my wife, Karen, and my editor, David Uhler, my special appreciation goes out to the pitchers who gave of their time, even when it wasn't convenient: Jeff Williams, Russ Peterich, Bonnie Robbins, Casey and Gail Sluys, Jerry Smith, and Kathy Loucks. And warmest thanks to Dave Loucks, who as president of the NHPA helped me in innumerable ways.

HISTORY OF HORSESHOES

Old Greek coins trace horseshoes—if not horseshoe pitching—to around 200 B.C. The Greeks, and later the Romans, shod their horses with iron plates and rings. Inevitably, some discus thrower wanna-bes took to heaving those discarded shoes.

Throwing a piece of metal or stone as a test of strength became known as quoits. At some point, quoits branched into discus throwing and a sport resembling horseshoe pitching. The latter was more a game of accuracy than strength, and as such was playable by more people.

Round plates for horses' hooves evolved into the horseshoe shape we know today, and the pitching of horseshoes moved across Europe during the sixteenth and seventeenth centuries, eventually becoming a favorite pastime in England. In eighteenth-century England, the class-minded rich viewed horseshoes as a vulgar, poor-man's version of quoits, which was seen as the proper, genteel game.

American colonists, ever eager to thumb their noses at aristocratic Brits, played a lot of horseshoes, transforming the game into a symbol of the common citizen. Benjamin Franklin is even said to have pitched a few shoes. Said the Duke of Wellington, nose angled skyward, "The colonial war of liberation was won on the village green by pitchers of horse hardware."

Horseshoe pitching was spread by other wars, too. Union soldiers in the Civil War passed the time tossing mule shoes in camp. After the war, courts sprang up in Union states, with everyone making up their own rules. Eventually, horseshoe courts were laid out in hundreds of cities, villages, and farming communities.

In 1869 quoit-pitching aficionados in England established rules for the game. The distance between stakes was set at 19

1

yards. Players, who stood level with the stakes, delivered their quoits with one step. Quoits could be any weight, but the outside diameter could not exceed 8 inches. The ground around the stakes was clay. Measuring distance for points was done from the closest part of the stake to the closest part of the quoit. These rules governed horseshoe pitching in the United States, too, but no records of tournaments predate 1909.

By the early twentieth century, the midwestern United States was the epicenter of the horseshoe world. The first U.S. horseshoe-pitching tournament open to the world was held in the summer of 1909 in Bronson, Kansas. Horseshoe historians consider that Year One of the World Horseshoe Pitching Tournament. At first the games were played on dirt courts with stakes 38 $\frac{1}{2}$ feet apart and only 2 inches above the ground. Games were played to twenty-one: ringers were worth five points, leaners three, and close shoes one point. There were no limits to shoe size or weight.

The first winner, Frank Jackson, was awarded a World Tournament belt with horseshoes dangling from it.

Although early records are sketchy, annual tournaments were apparently held in Missouri or Kansas for the next few years, with Jackson successfully defending his title as world champion each time.

Because the pitching rules differed from one location to another, top pitchers from Missouri and Kansas gathered in 1913 and agreed to adopt a uniform set of rules. Then someone asked the inevitable question: By what authority do these rules govern the game? In response, the organizers created the first ruling body for the game of horseshoes, the Grand League of the American Horseshoe Pitchers Association, founded in Kansas City, Kansas, in 1914. A constitution, bylaws, and rules were adopted and officers elected. The association granted charters to leagues in several states, and its rules governed all regular horseshoe-pitching tournaments. Rule changes, as detailed in its *Horseshoe Guide,* included raising the stakes to 8 inches and placing them 38 feet apart. Like value cancelled like value—that is, ringers cancelled ringers. The weight of shoes was standardized, so that by the 1915 tournament, all shoes weighed between 2 pounds and

2 pounds 2 ounces. Ringers counted five points, leaners three points, and closest shoe within 6 inches of the stake scored one point. Pitchers' boxes were 3 feet to either side of the stakes and 6 feet back; pitchers could stand anywhere in the box.

Another change was being wrought. For thousands of years, pitchers had thrown real horse hardware, burrs and all. But about this time sporting goods companies began making standard-size, smooth-surfaced, throwing shoes. This transformed pitching shoes into a game of skill rather than an exercise in masochism. (Throwing off-the-horse shoes, replete with abrasive burrs and nail holes, is somewhat akin to throwing large, heavy nail files.) Prior to this change, Shetland pony shoes sometimes had to compete against those of Clydesdales; now everyone was throwing essentially the same shoes, which made playing more equitable and competition more meaningful.

Prior to the twentieth century, whenever people picked up a shoe for the first time, they invariably grasped it by the butt, pointed the open end toward the stake, and threw, in the vain hope that it would stay in that position until it reached the stake. The trouble is, you have to have superhuman accuracy and control to heave a heavy horseshoe like a knuckleball and keep it dead-flat and dead-on-line; even if you could do it, the shoe would likely ricochet off the stake when the butt end hit.

Eventually, as with basketball's two-handed set shot, creative innovators caused the zero-turn throw to be consigned to the historical archives. One such innovator was Dr. Frank M. Robinson of Poughkeepsie, New York, who in 1909 began experimenting with a one-and-a-quarter turn. The advantages of a flat, turning shoe were apparent to those who watched Robinson finish second at the 1919 World Tournament. Rather than striking the stake straight on, Robinson's turning shoe darted around it, as though looking for an opportunity. If one of the forks caught the stake, with less impact than a straight-on shoe, it often stayed on.

There was an initial resistance to this newfangled technique, as though throwing too many ringers would somehow weaken the moral fiber of the nation. But, as always, those who stood still were left behind, and the game was soon dominated by pitchers throwing turning shoes.

Over the years, the game of horseshoes has also been dominated by North Americans, primarily from the United States, although six-time world champion Elmer Hohl of Ontario, Canada, would garner quite a few votes from the cognoscenti for Best Pitcher Ever. (He would get even more votes for Best Tournament Ever, for he was magic in 1968. He qualified for the World Tournament that year with an almost perfect two hundred shoes—572 points, only 28 shy of the maximum, and still a record. Then he blitzed the tournament field with thirty-five wins, no losses, and an 88.2 ringer percentage, another record that still stands.)

The combination of the turning shoe, the addition of hooks, or caulks, to horseshoes, and the repeated raising of the stake (2 inches in 1909; 6 inches in 1912; 8 inches in 1914; 10 inches in 1920; 12 inches in 1940; 14 inches in 1950) nudged ringer averages steadily upward. Harold Falor won the 1923 World Tournament with a 55 percent ringer average; Blair Nunamaker, the 1929 champion, hit 69.5 percent; and in 1940 four men broke the 80 percent mark for the first time. From then on, pitchers unable to average at least 80 percent would have no chance of winning the men's championship class. In 1968, nine pitchers at the World Tournament averaged 80 percent or more.

Today the National Horseshoe Pitchers Association of America (NHPA) is the governing body of horseshoe pitching. It organizes and promotes the sport, standardizes rules and equipment, and acts as a unifying agent for affiliated charters doing business in all fifty states, Japan, and Canada. Membership approaches twenty thousand, a fivefold increase since 1976, when Donnie Roberts first took over as chief administrator.

It's been said that Donnie Roberts was to horseshoes what Pete Rozelle was to football. Certainly both men presided over sports that enjoyed exponential leaps in popularity. Prior to Roberts, the NHPA served principally as a rule-making body and to arrange the annual World Tournament for a few elite competitors.

Under Roberts's regime, the rules of competition were changed, allowing greater participation at all levels. The 1994

World Tournament, for example, featured competition in 25 classes, from A to Y. In addition, there were age and gender flights, men's seventy-and-over, and girl's seventeen-and-under.

The result was more competition for more people. Pitchers who will never throw a 60 percent game now have at least a prayer of returning home the World Class E or R Horseshoe Champion. This has raised interest in both the World Tournament and the sport of horseshoes.

The growing popularity of horseshoes gave Roberts some leverage in trying to wring concessions from cities that are possible tournament sites. In 1980 he convinced Huntsville, Alabama, to build twenty-four lighted, nicely landscaped courts in a municipal park, with room for twenty-five hundred spectators. Huntsville hosted the 1980, 1982, and 1984 world championships.

Although the World Tournament is still dominated by Americans, the sport is enjoyed all over the world, including South Africa, Japan, Germany, Italy, Norway, Russia, Nigeria, Togo, Australia, Honduras, South America, Israel, and the Bahamas.

My advice to aspiring pitchers: Whenever you go abroad, practice saying, "Those are good shoes" in the local language.

COURT AND EQUIPMENT

··

Horseshoe pitching is refreshingly simple. You can do as little as shove two sticks into the ground and call it a court. But if you become at all serious about the game, if you want to see how good you can really be, you will have to start playing on regulation courts. And keep in mind that mediocre conditions favor weaker players. Quality courts reward merit and intensify competition.

GROUNDS

All you need to start is a fairly level plot of land about 10 feet wide and 50 feet long, free of trees, clotheslines, and electric wires. If possible, have it run north-south to keep the sun out of the pitchers' eyes. In the middle of the strip, drive two steel stakes in the ground, 40 feet from base to base. Then lean the stakes slightly toward each other, leaving 14 to 15 inches above ground. Till the soil around each stake, and throw down some sand if you have some.

Voila! You have constructed a perfectly adequate practice court (Fig.1). But let's say you want to build a regulation court, a replica of the courts you will see in tournaments. It should look like Figure 2.

If you construct multiple courts, remember to leave at least 12 feet between them, to maximize safety and concentration.

Clay. The ideal landing site for your shoes is synthetic or moist blue clay. If you choose the blue, keep a watering can around to wet it as needed. Experience will teach you when it's needed. The clay is at its best when it reaches a puttylike consistency that will stop a shoe on a dime. With clay, say good-bye to those halcyon backyard days when you slid the shoe onto the stake in a cloud of dust.

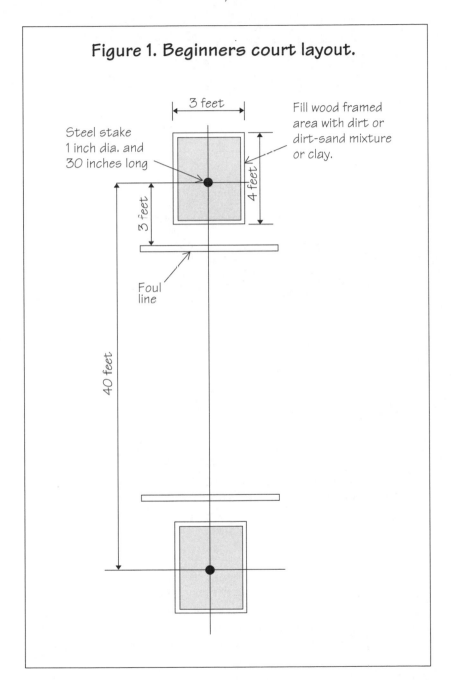

Figure 1. Beginners court layout.

3 feet

Fill wood framed area with dirt or dirt-sand mixture or clay.

Steel stake 1 inch dia. and 30 inches long

4 feet

3 feet

Foul line

40 feet

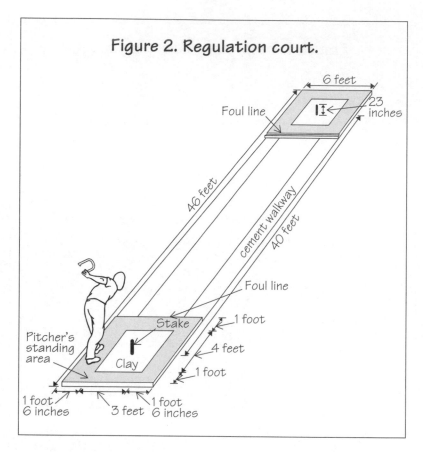

Figure 2. Regulation court.

Continuous sunshine can dry out clay so much that you may have to punch holes in it, and then pour water into the holes. During matches, it should be necessary only to wet the surface. After matches, give the clay a thorough soaking, then cover with damp burlap bags. Secure the bags by putting something heavy on the corners.

The Horseshoe Pro Shop, 1240 S. 17th St., Columbus, OH 43206-2973, has a product called Klean Klay, a synthetic clay developed especially for the sport of horseshoe pitching that needs no watering or shoveling. Rain water will not harm it. Simply cover it and keep it free of debris and it will last for years.

The following example should guide you in calculating how much synthetic clay you will need for your courts:

The minimum recommended depth of synthetic clay around each peg is 3 inches.

Each cubic foot of synthetic clay weighs 84 pounds.

Example: If your pit size is 36 inches by 48 inches, multiply 36 x 48 x 3 inches deep = 5,184 cubic inches. Then divide 5,184 by 1,728 (the number of cubic inches in 1 cubic foot) = 3 cubic feet. Finally, multiply 3 cubic feet x 84 pounds = 252 pounds of clay per end, or 504 pounds per court.

COURT EQUIPMENT

Stakes. The first task in equipping your court is to secure some stakes. If your stakes are long enough, you can just hammer them into the ground. Ringers will eventually work them loose, however, so it's better to buy a ready-built box with a welded stake. You can find both wood and synthetic portable courts, complete with backstops and synthetic clay at the above mentioned Horseshoe Pro Shop.

If you or someone you know is a welder, you can save money by making your own stakes from 27-inch long, 1-inch-diameter cold-rolled steel. The block in which the stake is inserted should be of 8-by-8-by-24-inch solid oak, treated with creosote or some other substance to protect against rot. The hole into which the stake is driven should be $^{15}/_{16}$-inch in diameter and 6 inches deep. Dip the bottom of the stake in motor oil to improve the fit, then drive the stake into the block, slip an iron plate over the stake, and attach with four lag screws (Fig. 3).

Backboards. It is recommended that you build some kind of backstop behind each stake to contain errant shoes—and there will be plenty of errant shoes. I've seen the shoes of topflight pitchers hit the top of a stake and ricochet over a 4-foot-tall cyclone fence. A backstop will help protect spectators who wander by with the misconception that horseshoe pitching is risk-free. It will also save beginners a lot of time searching for shoes.

The recommended specifications for backboards are as follows:

Height	12 inches
Width	3 feet
Distance behind peg	4 feet
Material	2 x 12 hardwood
Paint color	contrast stake color

If you don't want to use wood, the backstop can be made of heavy mesh, wire, belting, or any other material strong enough to withstand the pounding of your wild throws. Wire has the advantage of not obstructing the view of spectators, but then, just how many spectators were you expecting?

Figure 3. Set stake into wooden block or cement-filled container. Place container in ground, angle peg 3 inches toward opposite stake.

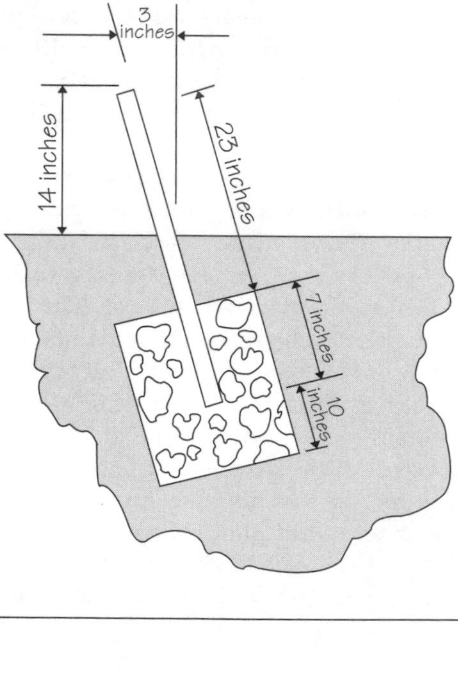

Figure 4. Court layout.

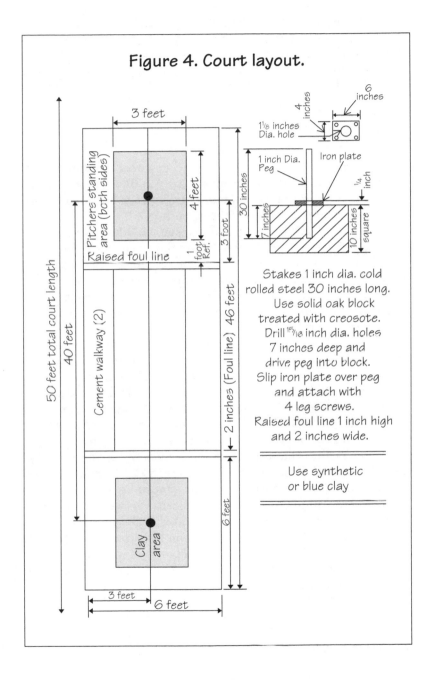

Stakes 1 inch dia. cold rolled steel 30 inches long. Use solid oak block treated with creosote. Drill $^{15}/_{16}$ inch dia. holes 7 inches deep and drive peg into block. Slip iron plate over peg and attach with 4 leg screws. Raised foul line 1 inch high and 2 inches wide.

Use synthetic or blue clay

Lighting. Courts can be lighted for night play very easily. For a single court, hang a flood lamp with a protective cover 8 to 12 feet above each stake. In addition to those two lights, the general area may be lighted with any suitable array of ordinary bulbs. Don't lose sight of the two main goals, reducing glare to a minimum and keeping the lights out of the players' eyes.

HORSESHOES

Horseshoes, like pitchers, come in different weights, dimensions, and tempers. Try different brands until you find one that works for you. Make sure you have a pair that fits your hand and needs. No two pitchers throw exactly the same way.

If you buy NHPA-approved shoes, you will likely pay between $18 and $68 per pair. Eighteen dollars buys you American brand shoes, which are perfectly adequate for beginners and beyond. At the other end of the spectrum are stainless steel shoes, such as Cal Flip, Greeott, and Star. Stainless steel shoes may not improve your score, but the skin of your fingers will appreciate their silky smooth surface.

Quality shoes come with a guarantee, from the lifetime guarantee of Diamond to six months for the M&M Special. Keep in mind that any shoe, if you pitch it long enough, will break.

Weight. A single horseshoe cannot weigh more than 2 pounds 10 ounces, but it can be as light as you want. Lighter shoes may seem easier to throw, but they are more likely to bounce off the stake. Heavier shoes will tend to be sucked into the clay.

If you're into counting grams of shoe weight, you probably already know that as the die wears out in the forging process, heavier shoes are produced; and that a mere $1/64$-inch difference in thickness will make a 1-ounce difference in weight. A coat of enamel paint or two coats of spray paint will also add an ounce to its weight and help reduce rebound from the stake. Clay stuck to a horseshoe can also add an additional ounce of weight.

Dimensions. A competitive horseshoe cannot exceed $7 1/4$ inches in width and $7 5/8$ inches in length, both outside measurements (Fig. 5). The shoe opening cannot exceed $3 1/2$ inches at a point $3/4$ of an inch from the heel points. A few hundred ringers can actually widen the gap. This should not, however, dissuade you from trying to throw ringers.

Figure 5. Anatomy of a horseshoe. The maximum weight of a horseshoe is 2 lb. 10 oz.

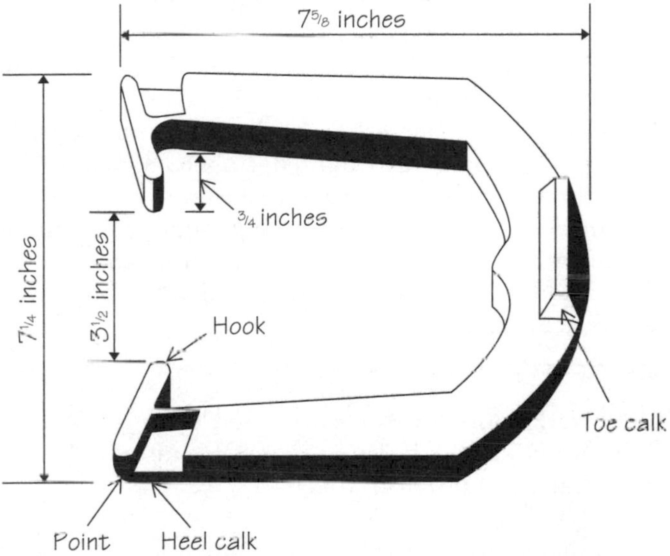

Tempers. The tips of horseshoes are case hardened, but in the middle, where the shoe is supposed to contact the stake, the metal may be soft, medium, or hard. Soft metals should ricochet less than hard metals, but soft tends to produce burrs that can rake your skin.

Look for horseshoes that fit your hand and feel comfortable. Try your friends' shoes. You may like more weight in the front of the shoe or the rear; you may like the feel of a particular shoe and not even know why.

PERSONAL EQUIPMENT

Clothing. As far as I know, *GQ* magazine has never done a spread on pitchers' fashions. And the rule book is mute on the subject of a dress code. Be guided by comfort. Shorts and jeans are fine. The shirt should provide freedom for the pitching arm to make its full arc, from high backswing to high follow-through, without constriction or irritation. T-shirts, bowling shirts, and polo shirts all serve the purpose.

As for footwear, look for soles that provide good traction. Pitching horseshoes is a game of inches, and wearing shoes that slip, slide, or turn even slightly can spell the difference between a ringer and a no-count shoe.

Accessories. No horseshoe pitcher is complete without a measuring tool, usually a straightedge about 8 inches long that will serve three purposes: as a ruler to measure whether a shoe is within 6 inches of the stake; as a straightedge to determine borderline ringers; as a scraper to remove clay from shoes.

You should also have a file for smoothing the abrasive burrs that can crop up on horseshoes.

> **T**he NHPA-approved Horseshoe Pitchers' Companion (write: 2058 Woods Circle, Barnhart, MO 63012) has the following features in one convenient tool:
> 1. Calipers for measuring close points.
> 2. File to remove burrs from shoes.
> 3. Six-inch notch for measuring scoring shoes.
> 4. Straightedge for measuring ringers.
> 5. Scraper for removing dirt
>   ... and it fits neatly into your back pocket!

Some players protect their fragile backs by retrieving their shoes from the pit with a metal hook.

You may also want to have score pads, percentage books, round-robin tournament schedules, and mastery summary charts, all of which are available through the NHPA.

Finally, if you pitch anywhere other than your home court, you will want to have some kind of carrying case for your equipment. You can make one or contact a representative of the NHPA (see "Resources") to find out where to buy one. A bowling bag will work; so will a fishing tackle box.

GRIP, STANCE AND SWING

··

GRIP

When you choose a grip, you are also deciding which turn you will use. The two most popular choices are the one-and-one-quarter and the one-and-three-quarters turns. Their names describe the number of turns the horseshoe makes in flight (clockwise for right-handers, counterclockwise for lefties). Any turn is permitted by the rules, and most of them work for someone.

Hand a beginner a shoe and ask him to toss it toward a stake, and chances are he will grab it by the curved end, point the open end at the stake, and flip it so that it turns end over end once or twice. This is called, appropriately, a "flip shoe."

Trouble is, the flip shoe has a nasty habit of bounding around like a crazed jackrabbit, sometimes for great distances. The loudest-clanging nonringers are often the booby prize of flip-shoe pitchers. In fact, no major tournament has ever been won by a 40-foot flip-shoe pitcher, although some juniors and women, who pitch from 30 feet, have achieved success with this technique.

Most serious 40-foot pitchers use a grip and delivery style that sends the horseshoe twirling on a horizontal plane, like a Frisbee. The key is to make the shoe turn slowly in flight so that the open end pirouettes around at just the right time to catch and hold the stake. If you have a good pitching arm, you may hit the stake more than half the time, but lacking that consistent, perfectly timed turn, your ringer percentage will hover around zero. On the other hand, once you find your turn, huge advances are possible.

In the early sixties, Ottie Reno polled 870 members of the National Horseshoe Pitchers Association (NHPA) and found that 94 percent used one of the open-shoe grips (498 pitched the one-and-one-quarter turn, 320 pitched the one-and-three-quarter turn, and only 8 pitched the flip).

Nevertheless, there is no absolutely right or wrong way to pitch a horseshoe. A man named Sol Berman started filming and taping accomplished pitchers in 1948, trying to spot reasons why some reached the top while others didn't; he detailed vast differences in technique among elite pitchers. One of the all-time greats, Curt Day, used a reverse three-quarters turn. Three-time world champion Dan Kuchcinski toured the country with a reverse one-and-one-quarter toss. Right-hander Casey Sluys, a 35 percent pitcher, pitches a reverse three-quarters turn, for the simple reason that a left-hander taught him how to pitch.

In the beginning, you would be wise to experiment with the various turns, eventually adopting the one that feels most comfortable. And you may decide to switch even after achieving some success. Russ Peterich, a 43 percent pitcher who wanted more, recently switched from the one-and-one-quarter turn to the one-and-three-quarters turn. Although he currently struggles with this new technique, he is confident that with it eventually he will surpass his previous level.

Whether you adopt the one-and-one-quarter turn, the one-and-three-quarters turn, the flip, or some eccentric toss, begin by emulating the techniques of the pros.

One-and-One-Quarter Turn

As with all pitching styles, your goal with the one-and-one-quarter-turn is to have the shoe land open at the stake. Direction and distance are also at issue, but you can usually solve those problems by throwing a lot of shoes. For many, orientation of the shoe is the most daunting challenge.

To pitch the one-and-one-quarter turn, grasp the shoe so that it is open to the left, with fingers below and thumb across the top of the blade. Start about halfway between the heel and toe, but be prepared to adjust the position of your hand as you assess your results. Keep the calks away from the body to assure that they land facing downward. The tips of the forefinger and middle finger should meet the thumb at the inner edge. The index, third, and fourth fingers normally grasp the shoe, with the pinky finger used for balance. Both the pinky and the third finger help level the shoe as it is released.

Figure 6. Grips.

1 ¼ turn grip

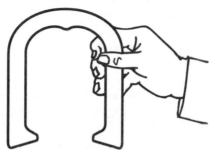

1 ¾ turn grip

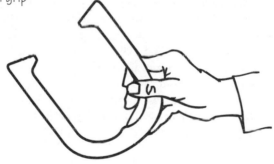

Flip shoe grip

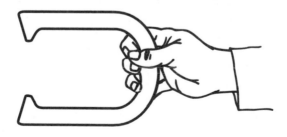

Don't flit from technique to technique without first giving each a chance. On the other hand, don't be afraid to experiment if change is called for. There are exceptions to every rule, and you may be one of them. Some accomplished pitchers have used a full-hand grip or held the shoe more toward the heel or toe. You are uniquely you; find what works best, your comfort zone.

One-and-Three-Quarters Turn

The second most popular turn is the one-and-three-quarters. The finger grouping is about the same as for the one-and-one-quarter, and the calks are again away from the body and thus facing down on release. But this time the fingers are placed on the opposite side of the shoe, so that the opening points to the right for right-handers or to the left for left-handers. The thumb rests on top of the blade and about 4 inches from the heel calk. The forefinger is wrapped around the underside of the shoe, about $2\,^3/_4$ inches from the heel hook, and the little finger rests against the toe calk. Again, pressure on the shoe is supplied by the thumb and forefinger, which release the shoe last. The turning motion is controlled by the earlier release of the middle finger.

Compared to the one-and-one-quarter turn, the one-and-three-quarters turn requires a little more wrist action, and slightly greater height to accommodate the extra half-turn.

Flip

Known also as a tumble shoe, the flip is the choice of most beginners. The shoe is held on the side opposite the opening, in the middle of the U, calks up, with the thumb next to the heel calk and the fingers on the opposite side. The movement of the flip is vertical rather than horizontal, end over end, tumbling once, twice, even three times, before reaching the stake.

The consensus of those in the know is that it's hard to be consistent from 40 feet with the flip. (As always there are exceptions: Jessie Gonzales was a longtime 80 percent pitcher with a flip shoe.) It does seem to have greater value, however, for some 30-foot pitchers.

No matter which turn you use, don't hold the shoe in a death grip. Pitcher and writer R. O. Brotherton likens the proper horseshoe grip to holding a handgun: "It's not necessary to hold it tightly, nor is it advisable to go to the other extreme."

STANCE

Your starting position is critical, for it sets the stage for all that follows. Most right-handed pitchers stand on the left platform (or to the left of the closest stake), as that puts their pitching arm in line with the target stake. If you set up even with the stake, you have 3 feet for your step before you reach the foul line. If you consistently come up, say, a foot short of the line, move forward 8 or 9 inches. You don't want to worry about the foul line, but you don't want to throw farther than necessary, either.

As you face the target, your feet should be fairly close together, toes pointed toward the stake. NHPA Hall of Famer Carl Steinfeldt points out that "nine out of ten (right-handers) will miss to the right. Left-handed players just the opposite. The reason for this is that the foot you pitch off of is not lined up with the other peg." Beginners, especially, are likely to point their toes several degrees away from the target peg. If that describes you, then straighten your feet so they are pointed right at the peg. That way, when the arm flows past the leg, it will automatically be in line with the target.

Your body should be fairly upright and balanced, without too much forward lean. Test your balance by having someone nudge you from the side or back—it shouldn't displace you.

It's a matter of personal preference whether to have one foot slightly ahead of the other. Right-handers who put their left foot forward effectively shorten their stride; if they drop their left foot back, they lengthen their potential stride. Experiment with various positions, then adopt the one that is most comfortable for you. Stay with it until you become convinced that it isn't right.

SWING

Address. Whether you call it addressing the stake, taking aim, sighting, getting a bead on the target, or something else, there is a critical moment of preparation just before you begin delivery. Some pitchers hold the shoe in front of their face and look through or over it; others hold it near their chest, over their head, beside their ear, or down at their side, all the while staring at the target stake.

The goal of the address is to see the target and to develop a feel for the shoe so that your delivery is natural and easy. With that in mind, Carl Steinfeldt discourages young pitchers from bringing the shoe up in front of their face and holding it motionless, letting the hand and forearm muscles get tense and stiff. Instead, he suggests, take a deep breath and let it out. "If the air is in your body you are stiff and tense," he says. "By letting the air out before you swing, you are loose and limber." Then bring the shoe up briefly, let it drop down to the side, and take a practice swing up and back, nice and loose, like a baseball hitter taking shadow swings.

Step. Right-handers will normally step with the left foot as they pitch. A notable exception was Jim Solomon, a former Pennsylvania state champion who was capable of throwing 80 percent ringers coming off the "wrong" foot.

Prior to the step, body weight should be equally distributed between both feet, or in such a way that the pitcher feels balanced. Then body weight shifts to the right foot (for left-footed steppers), just as if you were starting to walk.

Here again, individual differences abound. Some accomplished pitchers rely on a short stride, others on a much longer one. You will have to find what works for you, but in general guard against overstriding. And don't abandon the stride altogether, for the shift of weight from back foot to front foot lends power to your delivery.

The forward step begins while the arm is still busy with the backswing, but it shouldn't be completed until well after the arm starts forward.

Dave Loucks, who has photographed and studied many top pitchers, says that the typical right-hander has a pronounced

Figure 7. Sighting through the shoe works well for some pitchers.

crossover step, with the left foot ending up in front of the right foot, causing the pitcher to miss right. "In my case, I have a stride that flies open toward the opposite platform, and I miss left," he explains. "But I'm the exception. Whether you miss left or right, the step is often the root cause of problems, particularly for beginners."

Backswing. Once you have chosen a grip, assumed a stance, and addressed the stake, it's time to start the backswing. It's also

Figure 8. Most right-handers step with the left foot.

a good time to burn the KISS acronym into your brain—Keep It Simple, Stupid.

Relax your body. Stay loose and limber. Take a deep breath and let it out, like a basketball player before a foul shot. Drop the shoe down to your side, then bring it up and back, up and back, nice and fluid. Imagine your backswing describing a half-circle.

During the backswing, the body starts to lean forward at the hips. Don't rush. Make sure you hesitate slightly at the top of the backswing just before the start of the forward swing. A hurried backswing can throw your step and forward swing out of synchronization, which often leads to short and unopened shoes.

Figure 9. Some excellent pitchers have big backswings, but comfort should determine how far back you carry the shoe.

Now you have a decision to make—how far behind your body should you carry the shoe? Pay attention to your body—arm, torso, even legs—for it will provide the answer. Allow your pitching arm to go only as far back as is comfortable. If you go farther than that, you will lose balance, and hence accuracy.

Experiment with different backswing arcs to determine which one is best for you. Note your results.

One of the greatest right-handed pitchers who ever lived, Elmer Hohl, visualized an imaginary stake about 1 to $1\frac{1}{2}$ inches to the left of the real stake. Carl Steinfeldt, who has taught countless pitchers, subscribes to this technique and advises others to do the same. Because a right-handed shoe twists in from the left, missing left gives the pitcher the entire $3\frac{1}{2}$-inch opening as a margin of error. If, on the other hand, a right-hander misses to the right, the shoe is past the stake and has no chance to latch on to it. Left-handers should place their imaginary stake on the right of the real stake.

Forward Swing. Now that you've brought your arm back to a predetermined spot behind your body and hesitated ever so slightly, it's time to bring it forward. As the pendulum starts to swing forward, you will take a step with the foot opposite your pitching arm. Carl Steinfeldt believes that for many pitchers the arm lags behind the step. If the foot moves forward and plants while the shoe is still back at the end of the backswing, he says, the pitching arm will be stiff. Try to have the shoe starting forward on its downward arc before your foot touches the ground. "If you do that," says Steinfeldt, "it will make that forty feet seem like thirty-nine."

As the shoe passes your right leg (right-handers) on its way forward, your hand and forearm begin to rotate clockwise to a nearly palm-up position. Your weight shifts forward, the horseshoe goes from vertical to horizontal, and it is released somewhere between your chest and eyes. As you near the release point, your arm, wrist, and hand are parallel to the ground.

Don't forget that old-time rhythm. Like bowlers and softball pitchers, horseshoe pitchers must maintain a smooth, well-oiled swing.

Release. Everyone's stride and stroke is a little different, so you will have to experiment to find your precise release point. In terms of height, you should release the shoe when the opposite peg appears in the center of the shoe. Since your arm swing is to the side of your body, you can't see this during competition. Try it in practice until you firmly establish a mental picture and physical sensation of the height of the release.

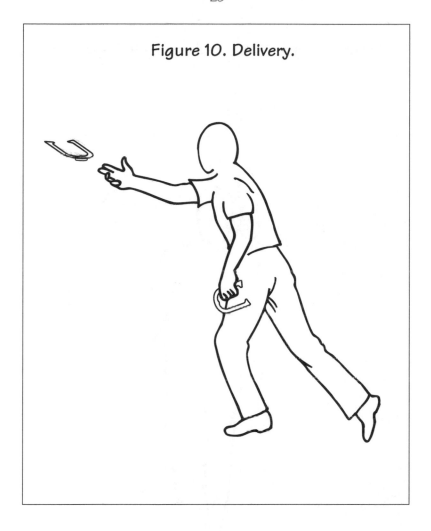

Figure 10. Delivery.

Most pitchers, especially beginners, release the shoe between the waist and the chest. If you have a pronounced forward lean, as some topflight pitchers do, your release point will be closer to shoulder height. Once you find the optimum release point, try to attain it with each throw. Work for a clean release, free of twists, jerks, or finger drag.

Other important variables include height and trajectory of the pitch. The apex of the arc will probably be between 7 and 10 feet. The idea is to make the shoe land flat and dead and open.

Figure 11. A good follow-through is important.

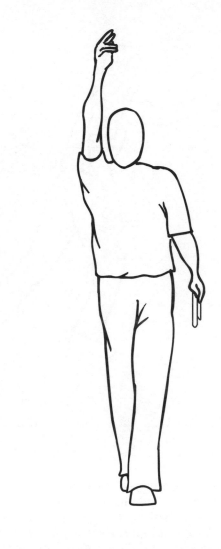

Pitch too low and the shoe doesn't have time to open properly; moreover, it must be propelled faster to reach the stake, increasing the chances of rebound. Pitch the shoe too high, and it will hang too long in the air and turn farther than it should. In general, it's best to miss high rather than low. The shoe is more likely to stay put when it lands. Besides, if it fails to reach the stake, it has almost no chance of being a ringer. As many a golfer has muttered: "Never up, never in."

Some points to remember:

1. To vary the amount of turn, move the grip up or down the blade.
2. Keep your eyes continuously on the target stake during the pitch.
3. Try to throw all shoes the same height. Low shoes tend to be short shoes; shoes thrown too high make it difficult to judge distance.
4. A little wobble during flight is desirable to ease the landing. A pitch without wobble tends to land hard and rebound.
5. Try to land the shoe heel calk first.
6. At first, strive for the proper turn rather than for ringers. When the turn comes, remember the grip and stay with it.

The turn of the shoe is accomplished by a roll of the forearm. When the shoe is at your side, it's in a more-or-less vertical position; as your arm starts forward, the forearm roll turns it toward the horizontal. The amount of turn is increased by waiting longer to level the shoe, and decreased by doing it sooner. Unlike a football pass, a released horseshoe should have a little wobble to slow the shoe's speed and reduce bounce-back from the stake.

Follow-through. The follow-through is the final stage of the pitching motion. During this stage, the finishing touch is put on the pitch. It is a mistake to terminate the forward swing abruptly just because the shoe has left your hand. In other words, stifle the little voice in your head that says the shoe is gone and nothing you do now is going to make any difference.

Remember, a short, low shoe was released too soon. On the other hand, if you hang onto a shoe too long, it will lose directional authority.

As you release, try to imagine your arm "reaching for the stake." This will assure a good follow-through, giving your shoe more authority and direction. At the point of release, don't stop or jerk your hand; rather, let it continue upward in a natural arc.

It simply doesn't make sense to strive for a smooth, coordinated backswing, forward swing, and release, only to chop it off the moment the shoe is gone. Just as backswing is connected to foreswing, release is connected to follow-through. A good follow-through can provide the lift you will need to guide a horseshoe 30 or 40 feet to its target.

Let's put the entire swing together: After aligning yourself with the target stake, sight over the top of your shoe; take a deep breath and visualize success; to start your delivery, push your arm out and up, then let it drop and swing as far back as it will naturally go; start the lift at the bottom of your swing, letting the shoe go when your hand is about at the level of the top of the opposite peg.

Videotape yourself pitching and have a good pitcher analyze your form. Use the slow-motion feature of your camcorder to help you pick out mistakes, such as not keeping your wrist straight, dropping the shoulder of your pitching arm, or varying the height of your throws.

Now practice this until the horses come home and want their shoes back. After that, practice "shadow pitching" in front of a mirror until you can vividly picture the entire swing. Feel the shoe during all phases of the swing. Let the arm do its thing without interruption or interference from the conscious mind.

STRATEGY

······································

There are several steps you can take to help your game, even though they have nothing to do with developing a better swing.

TAKE ADVANTAGE OF YOUR FOUL LINE

Horseshoe pitching has compensatory factors built into the game that allow players of disparate abilities to play one another. Giving points to the weaker player is one form of handicapping; another is allowing women, juniors, and elders (players over seventy) to pitch from 30 feet, 10 feet closer than the open men. This is a controversial rule, and many of the letters to the editor of the NHPA magazine, *Newsline,* are filled with emotional arguments for and against allowing 30-foot pitchers to compete against 40-foot pitchers.

We refer to them as 30-foot and 40-foot pitchers, but because the foul lines are 3 feet in front of each stake, they are actually 27-foot and 37-foot pitchers. Yet many beginners start even with the stake, take one step, and finish a foot or more short of the foul line. Why not take everything the rules give you? Move forward, experiment with your starting point, and try to finish a couple of inches short of the line instead of a foot or two. This will help you avoid the heartbreak of short shoes.

When you finally find a spot that works for you, hold on to it; try to release every shoe from the same position every time. Accuracy depends upon true consistency.

LEARN TO PITCH TO OTHER RINGERS

Walter Ray Williams, Jr., says that he aims about 4 inches up the stake. Why he says exactly 4 inches is unclear, but the important point is that if you hit partway up the stake, you have a chance for a ringer—in Williams's case, a very good chance—while on clay you have no chance if you hit short.

Whether or not you employ Walter Ray's technique when the pit is empty, you should definitely aim higher than ground level when your opponent has already thrown a ringer or two. For if your shoe comes in low and hits the steel of your opponent's shoe, it can easily ricochet away. Hit high on the stake and you have a better chance of holding a ringer.

Recently, the best pitchers in the world, Walter Ray Williams, Jr., and Alan Francis, competed in a match that went 136 shoes. Francis threw 129 ringers and scored forty-one points. Walter Ray threw 121 ringers (89 percent) but scored only fifteen points. Talk about having to play other ringers!

FOCUS ON YOUR GAME

Talk to accomplished athletes in just about any sport and you will hear of the importance of concentration, but in no sport is it more important than horseshoes. That's because if you compete in tournaments, you will have to pitch side-by-side with other players. For example, at the 1995 Northern California Regionals, eighty pitchers went at it simultaneously on forty tightly packed courts. The quality of play was excellent, so chatter was low and clanging was high. It sounded like a restaurant during a busy lunch.

If you're going to compete in tournaments, you have to block out the other pitchers. In fact, you need to shield yourself from any sensory stimuli that don't help you throw more ringers. The goal, if you take the game seriously, is to become a robotic pitcher, an automaton that does the same thing every time. People who try to describe the pitching style of Walter Ray Williams, graceful though he might be, inevitably conclude that "That guy's a machine."

Carl Steinfeldt is one of many pitchers who concentrate by

ignoring their opponent. "My aim is to average between eight and nine ringers out of every ten shoes," he says. "I know if I do that, my opponent is not going to do much off me. It keeps my mind on my own game and not on his."

Russ Peterich, who is profiled in the "Getting Better" chapter, agrees. He is a four-year, 43 percent pitcher who came to horseshoes from a baseball background. He says the hardest thing for him to overcome was the tendency to compete against other people. "My first couple of years when my opponent would get a ringer or two, I'd think, 'Oh, I've got to top that ringer or my opponent's going to get the points.' Now I've changed my approach. The most important thing is to hit the peg every time. I'm really playing against myself, trying to improve my percentage. I don't care what the other person does. If he makes four or five ringers in a row, I can't start getting nervous, or pretty soon I'm falling apart. Concentration is blown and now I'm playing even worse."

No matter what tricks you use to help you focus, don't forget the most basic one of all: Keep an unwavering eye on the target. Continue to watch the part of the stake you're aiming for—even after the shoe is in flight. Said former Pennsylvania champion Jim Soloman, "In this way I am aware only of the stake. It helps to keep out of my mind all interferences, the spectators, my opponent, the score, or the situation."

PLAY AT YOUR PACE

Some players work a lot more quickly than others. The rules let you take up to thirty seconds to release both shoes. Some players, like Jeff Williams, may be done in ten seconds, while others consistently take twenty-nine seconds. At the top level, players regularly try to coax opponents out of their natural rhythm. Fast players try to speed up slower players, and vice versa. Kathy Loucks, who considers herself one of the fastest players, admits that she sometimes tries to derail opponents psychologically. "If someone plays slow, I might walk quickly to the other stake, pick up my shoes quickly, call the score quickly," she says. "Of course, a good player will just ignore that and not be taken out of her game."

Although this technique is seen more often at advanced levels, even beginners can subtly influence their opponents in similar ways. At the very least, don't let your opponent take you out of your rhythm.

GROW OLD

All you have to do is turn seventy and they let you move up 10 feet to pitch. A few proud and fit septuagenarians have declined the opportunity to throw from 30 feet, but most accept time's erosion of their skills and move closer.

Let's say the horseshoe spirit is still alive, but injury or age prevents you from walking back and forth, stake to stake. You can play a version of the game called Four Shoes, in which Player "A" stays at one stake, Player "B" at the other. Player "A" pitches all four shoes at his opponent's stake. After Player "B" counts his opponent's points, he then pitches all four back to Player "A," and so forth. The game is played to twenty-one points, with Player "B" having last pitch if "A" went first. With no walking, the only exertion is bending over to pick up shoes. An angler's gaff hook or a slender piece of 3-foot wire bent at one end to form a hook will reduce the bends.

WINNING
THE MENTAL GAME

·······································

You will inevitably master the physical skills of horseshoes before the mental ones. When learning a new sport, we tend to concentrate on the muscular activities, which is as it should be. Only after finding a grip and developing a swing can you begin to play the mental game. First you learn to hit the stake, then you learn to "think" in horseshoes.

Even as a recreational hacker, mastering the so-called inner game of horseshoes can give you a competitive advantage. If you mentally fortify yourself with the techniques in this chapter, you can become a better pitcher—without throwing a single shoe. Strive for the three C's: consistency, confidence, and, especially, concentration.

CONCENTRATION

If you talk to accomplished athletes in any sport, you will hear them speak of the importance of concentration. Sometimes called focus, it's at the heart of success in any endeavor, whether it's Cajun cooking, brain surgery, or tossing slabs of metal at a stake.

Most everyone knows that concentration has to do with paying attention. Does that mean consciously willing yourself to focus? Is concentration a shrill voice in your head screaming over and over, "Pay attention!" until you do? Maybe at first.

Focus is delicate, elusive. Pay close attention to the trees and you may miss the forest, and vice versa. Eventually, if you stay with it, you will learn to relax and focus more naturally. Once you groove a swing, you may be able to turn game control over to your now well-developed instincts, your subconscious.

Your conscious mind, however, will want to interfere. Consider this athletic equation:

$$Performance = Potential - Interference$$

Hall of Famer Carl Steinfeldt on concentration: "The hardest part in becoming an 'A' player is concentration. What I have done for the past fifty years to block the other player from my mind is to keep track of how many ringers I make every ten pitches. Also, [I] never talk to an opponent during a game. If you miss a ringer you have forty feet to walk and think about what you did wrong."

Performance is how well you actually do—your results; potential is a measurement of the best performance you are capable of at any given moment; interference is the mental static produced by the conscious mind. When pressure is minimal, the mind may become distracted: "Wonder what Ashley is doing. . . . How about those Giants? . . . Boy, do I look stunning in these jeans and cowboy boots!"

As pressure mounts, so do self-doubts and anxiety, two other prime causes of mental static. Again, the conscious mind rushes in, usually with a litany of advice: "Align yourself . . . address the stake . . . nice and loose . . . slow backswing . . . good release . . . follow through . . . oops!"

With all that advice raining down on you, is it any wonder that you're tighter than this year's budget? And what happens when you're tight? The unwanted contraction of even a few muscle fibers in the arms is enough to turn the shoe off line a few degrees, transforming a ringer into a bad shoe.

A reduction of mental interference will improve performance, even with no change in potential (read: *practice*). In other words, get your head screwed on right and you can become a better player without even picking up a shoe.

But the overactive conscious mind does not react well to being told to butt out. (It's rather like ordering yourself to sleep.) Instead, you will have to rely on deceit. Some athletic coaches suggest distracting the conscious mind by focusing on something only marginally related to the task at hand. By giving it something else to chew on, the subconscious is left unfettered. Two ways to distract that pesky conscious mind are by positive association and visualization; you can also "swing by the numbers."

Associate Positively. To associate positively, immerse yourself in positive recollections. Suppose you are pitching for the match, and you need a ringer. Like everyone, you've had both good and bad moments in the past. For best results, embrace the successes and discard the failures. Replay an imaginary tape you might call "My Greatest Hits."

Visualize. First cousin to positive association, visualization is a type of mental rehearsal in which you conjure up detailed visions of the activity before you do it.

The first step in visualization is to relax. Use a method that works for you. You might close your eyes and take a few deep breaths, recite your favorite mantra, or play a mental videotape of a winning moment. You may visualize from your own perspective or from that of your favorite omniscient being—whatever works.

Focus on the finer points of the swing. Immerse yourself in the swing. See it as one fluid whole. Feel the heft of the shoe, the fingers curling around the steel shaft; see it flying toward the target; hear the satisfying chink it makes as it wraps itself around the stake.

Visualization takes dedicated practice. The upside is that you can practice it anywhere—in a bed or bathtub, at a bus stop—and the rewards can be staggering. I have interviewed and profiled forty-two world-class athletes, and most attribute some, if not most, of their success to visualization.

Research suggests that muscles respond to visualization of an act almost as if you did the act. Thus, the more intensely you visualize the perfect pitch, the more entrenched it will be in your muscle memory. This kind of memory operates almost entirely on the subconscious level, which helps explain how you can play well but can't tell others how to do it.

The power of visualization received a lot of publicity in the seventies with the revelations of several famous athletes. Golfer Jack Nicklaus said that he never hit a shot without first seeing the ball's perfect flight followed by its "sitting up there high and white and pretty on the green." A successful shot, according to Nicklaus, was 50 percent visualization, 40 percent setup, and only 10 percent swing.

Swing by the Numbers. Whether or not positive association or visualization works for you, there is a third technique you can try. Count, aloud or silently, to three: "one" on the first forward swing, "two" as your pitching arm goes back, and "three" on the forward swing and release. Try to synchronize the sound with the action. It's harder than you might think, and the conscious mind should be fully engaged trying to accomplish it. You may find that counting lends your swing a rhythm it previously lacked.

ATTITUDE

Pitching horseshoes is a great test for anyone who seeks to improve his or her temperament, because to succeed means to be steady of temperament. The mental rigors of the sport seem to weed out the seething volcanic types; tempers rarely flare in horseshoes.

The time before a match should be spent limbering up—both physically and mentally. The biggest difference between the competent and the excellent in any sport is mental preparation. Successful athletes find a way to remain, or quickly regain, calm. To be effective, you must keep a check on counterproductive emotions. Some play better than others when they're mad; no one plays well in a rage. Analyze missed shots, but don't dwell on them.

Wally Amos, founder of Famous Amos Cookies, has ricocheted between rags and riches. An expert in both success and failure, he offers seven important qualities necessary for success in any pursuit.
1. Patience.
2. Acceptance.
3. Focus.
4. Commitment.
5. Enthusiasm.
6. Positive attitude.
7. Honesty and integrity.

Rhys Thomas, a nationally ranked croquet player, suggests three kinds of athletic cruelty.
1. The cruelty of opponent versus opponent.
2. The cruelty of nature—what the weather or court can do to you.
3. The cruelty you inflict upon yourself—inner cruelty.

PRESSURE

As you improve and face stiffer competition, the pressure mounts. It is pressure that causes a good pitcher to toss an air-shoe two feet short of the stake. Succumbing to pressure choking is a risk for any athlete, but it's especially an issue for horseshoe pitchers; after you reach a certain skill level, the game becomes more head than arm.

The competitive format of horseshoes intensifies the pressure. Cancellation scoring, the most common system, enables a competitor to affect his opponent's score. If, for example, the first pitcher throws two ringers, the second pitcher can cancel one or both by throwing his own ringers. High-level matches, then, are not so much won as lost by the first player to crack under pressure.

Picture this scenario: You're behind in a match against a pretty good player in your neighborhood or club. You have to hit two ringers to stay in the game. There are a few people watching and you feel the rivalry. Your guts are twisting like wet rope. Now that's pressure. Most everyone feels it at one time or another. The real question is whether you can control it. Successful people don't dodge pressure; they make it work to their benefit.

On the other hand, some seem to be able to block it out entirely. The mental tenacity of pitchers Carl Steinfeldt and Elmer Hohl were on display in 1964, when they combined to throw fifteen consecutive *four-deads,* a world record that still stands.

When horseshoers gather around the pickle barrel to discuss mental tenacity, the name Curt Day often comes up. Day, a Hoosier, won fourteen straight Indiana titles from 1959 to 1972, with a 147–5 match record. He was, according to Donnie Roberts, levitated to a new level by competition. "The thing about Curt was that competition seemed to lift up his game," says Roberts. "There was absolutely no quit to him. You had a feeling he was a bulldog fastened onto your leg."

Successful pitchers are able to whistle up that bulldog when they need it.

And then there's George Brett, destined for the Baseball Hall of Fame, who had pressure in perspective. When asked about the pressure of playing his sport, he said, as I paraphrase it, "Pressure? Ha, this isn't pressure. This is just a game. Pressure is feeding a family of four on a fixed income."

GETTING BETTER

··

L ike many sports, horseshoes suffers from an image problem. Mention horseshoe pitching to most people and they picture a couple of hayseeds in overalls chucking shoes behind the barn.

Actually, though, contemporary horseshoe aficionados span the socioeconomic spectrum. And if it's played correctly—that is, with skill—it is a game that demands exceptional endurance, power, and mental tenacity. Doubters should consider Don Titcomb, a skilled pitcher who had all of those traits. He won the 1960 World Championship by pitching six hours a day for six consecutive days in brutal Indiana heat and humidity. In all, he threw 2,878 shoes (4 tons), of which 2,443 (almost 4 tons) held the stake, a ringer percentage of 84.9.

If you become serious about pitching horseshoes, try to advance your game both on and off the court. Play lots of games, throw lots of shoes, but also maintain a workout regimen focused on enhancing the skills needed to become the best horseshoe pitcher in the world—or at least on your block.

Seek out opponents and partners who are slightly better than you, who will demonstrate new techniques and skills. Beating up on weaker players may briefly fuel your feelings of superiority, but it won't help you improve nearly as much as some hard-fought, well-played, learning-intensive defeats. Against good opponents, you will learn how to think under pressure; you will also learn how hard it can be to score even when pitching well.

Work on your weaknesses. If, for example, you are throwing short, confront that head on. Go back to the basics. Analyze your stance, swing, release point, and follow-through.

Set high standards for yourself. Don't assume that you've attained perfection just because you unleash two good ones in a row. Can you throw five in a row? Practice until you can.

There's the old story of the Texans driving through New York on their way to a concert. They stop to ask directions.

"How do you get to Carnegie Hall?" they ask an old man.

"Practice . . . practice," he answers.

PRACTICE

You've been hearing it since you were a kid: "If you want to improve, you have to practice." Indeed, it is the willingness to practice that separates the masters from the middling, no matter what the pursuit. As sports philosopher George Leonard says, "The master of any game is generally a master of practice."

The master's journey begins as soon as you commit to learning a new skill—whether it's growing cucumbers in bottles or playing mah-jongg. But sports provide an especially effective launching pad for the pursuit of excellence, mostly because the results of training are clearly visible. In most sports, you can plot your progress, either with statistics or by comparing yourself to other players. In horseshoes, your ringer percentage, like a batting average in baseball, is a clear and tidy way of measuring progress.

It's important to understand that the master's journey is not an inexorably upward slope. Instead, it is composed of brief spurts of progress, each followed by a slight decline to a plateau usually somewhat higher than the previous plateau.

Clearly, then, you have to be prepared—and content—to spend a lot of time on plateaus; you have to push yourself to practice even when no progress is evident. Only with diligent practice will you ingrain the pitch in muscle memory, the behavioral autopilot that works on the subconscious level.

Carl Steinfeldt, among others, suggests using two pairs of shoes when you practice. One pair is yours and the other pair, arranged as ringers, belongs to a competitor who regularly beats you.

Even if you're bursting with talent, practice is essential; in fact, you may have to practice harder because we tend to ease up when skills come easily. We're tempted, in George Leonard's words, "not to penetrate to the marrow of a practice." Instead of being frustrated with plateaus, learn to revel in them. If you can enjoy them as much as the upslopes, you are on the path to mastery.

Former champion Don Titcomb used to have a three-month training regimen for a world tournament. He would throw one hundred shoes a day for the first month, two hundred a day for the second month, between three hundred and four hundred a day for the third month, then take a week's rest before the tournament. Although horseshoe pitchers don't practice as much as gymnasts or ice skaters, the good ones believe in practicing every day, or nearly so.

According to George Leonard, author of *Mastery*, there are five keys to opening the doors to mastery:
1. Instruction: Be open to first-rate teaching.
2. Practice: Think of the word as a noun, not just a verb, as something you are, not just something you do.
3. Surrender: Give in to your teacher and the demands of your discipline.
4. Intentionality: Muster all the mental energy and vision you can behind the pursuit.
5. The Edge: Push yourself beyond your ordinary limits.

OBSERVE OTHERS

We generally learn new skills and improve old ones by doing, listening, and watching. If you are out of touch with competitive horseshoes, contact a local club (see "Resources") and observe pitchers who are better than you. Later, you might be able to work as a scorekeeper or a judge. In either case, you are a captive audience.

KEEP SCORE

If you play serious horseshoes, you will probably do some score keeping. Many elite pitchers have improved their game by keeping score for others. It's an ideal opportunity to sit in the catbird seat and study the dynamics of a match. The job forces you to focus. You can watch and evaluate mechanics, strategy, players' strengths and weaknesses, the rise and fall of pressure and how the players handle it—all the while keeping a written record, a distillation of what works and what doesn't.

If you do keep score, do it right. A study of 5,700 score sheets from the 1994 World Tournament uncovered 2,565 errors. Yet proper scoring procedure is not very complicated.

The score is called out to the scorekeeper at the end of each inning by the player who has scored.

The proper calls are shown on the accompanying table.

Call	Ringers Column		Inning Points	
No score			–	–
1 ringer each no score	X	X	–	–
4 Dead	XX	XX	–	–
1 ringer each 1 point	X'	X	1	–
1 point			1	–
2 points			2	–
1 ringer 3 points	O		3	–
3 ringers 3 points	XO	X	3	–
1 ringer 4 points	O'		4	–
2 ringers 6 points	OO		6	–

Figure 12 shows how a typical NHPA game score sheet looks for a game played under cancellation scoring.

Figure 12. Score Sheet.

SCORE SHEET	CALL	Ringers Column	Inning Points
	No score	X ┊ X	— —
	1 ringer each no score	XX ┊ XX	— —
	4 Dead	X ┊ X	1 —
	1 ringer each one point	┊	1 —
	1 point	┊	2 —
	2 points	O ┊	3 —
	1 ringer 3 points	XO ┊ X	3 —
	3 ringers 3 points	O ┊	4 —
	1 ringer 4 points	OO ┊	6 —
	2 ringers 6 points		

Class _____ Date _____

Game # _____ Court _____

#___ _____ Vs. # ___ _____

Ringers	Points	Score	Shoes	Ringers	Points	Score
			Handicap			
			2			
			4			
			6			
			8			
			10			
			12			
			14			
			16			
			18			
			20			
			22			
			24			
			26			
			28			
			30			
			32			
			34			
			36			
			38			
			40			
			42			
			44			
			46			
			48			
			50			
			52			
			54			
			56			
			58			
			60			
			62			
			Single Points			
			Points			
			Ringers			
			Shoes Pitched			
			Percentage			

Scorekeeper _____

JUDGE

Occasionally, when competitors can't resolve a difference of opinion, they have to call out a referee, a "judge" in official parlance.

According to the NHPA, these are the steps to follow when two contestants call for you to settle a dispute:

1. Ask what the contestants want determined.
2. Ask whether they agree on the nonrelevant shoes.
3. Remove those shoes.
4. Measure the shoes in question and make your determination.
5. Announce your decision.

When measuring for a point or a ringer, you may need to dig out the clay surrounding the shoe or the stake. Follow these procedures:

1. Be careful not to move either shoe or stake; don't lean on the stake.
2. Pack clay around the edges of the shoe to keep it from moving.
3. Prop up a precariously leaning shoe with clay, being careful not to displace it.
4. Dig gently to avoid disturbing the position of the shoes.

Is the shoe a ringer or just closest to the stake? Take the following steps to render that decision:

1. Verify which shoe is closest to the stake in case the shoe in question is not a ringer.
2. Span from point to point of the shoe with a straight edge, noting whether or not it touches the stake.

Once you have rendered your decision, walk away and avoid debate. If the contestants don't agree with you, they can lodge a protest with the league or the tournament committee.

EXPERT ADVICE

Ottie W. Reno, horseshoe writer and pitcher, offers these sugges-
tions for becoming a complete pitcher:

1. Control emotions. Strive to be cool at all times, and if
   you don't feel cool, fake it.
   Threats to your cool are everywhere: bad conditions,
   noisy spectators, unethical opponents, yesterday's traf-
   fic accident, the injustice of good throws bouncing off
   the stake. But you will not master horseshoes until you
   master your own temperament.
2. Find a rhythm. Sometimes called a zone, this is a mental space that allows you to perform at your best. Some
   have described it as a form of self-hypnosis. However
   you describe it, things are flowing as they should be.
3. Develop and maintain a competitive edge. Practice is
   essential, but you must compete to get better. Nothing
   hones pitching skills like pitching on top of double
   ringers, knowing that each miss means three points for
   your opponent.
4. Set goals and keep records. In the absence of specific
   goals, both practice and game time are wasted aimlessly. Have a purpose with each throw, even if it's just
   to do your best. Keep records so you don't kid yourself.
   Ringer percentage makes it easy to set incrementally
   higher goals. Gail Sluys, who qualified as a rookie at 13
   percent, decided that each year she would shoot for the
   next percentage that was divisible by ten. Sure enough,
   she finished her second year at 20 percent, her third
   year at 30 percent, and stayed on schedule until 1994,
   when she topped 70 percent.
5. Make the most out of practice. Establish a regular practice schedule and try to adhere to it.
   Never practice aimlessly, without trying to do your
   best. Bad practice habits will carry over into games.
   If you aren't mentally prepared to concentrate, don't
   practice.

6. Build confidence. Of course, it normally takes success to build confidence. But success is relative—a 10 percent ringer average may be exhilarating progress to a novice. Use each plateau as a stepping stone to a new level.

7. Learn to handle pressure. Pressure, too, is relative. You may feel it in your backyard when you are losing to someone you expected to beat. Good pitchers thrive on pressure; the rest of us have a tendency to fold up like cheap lawn chairs.

8. Correct mistakes. Great pitchers seldom make the same mistake twice in a row. They learn from their error and adjust accordingly.

9. Be courteous and ethical. Stand at the rear of the pitcher's box while your opponent pitches. Make no sound or motion that will disturb his or her concentration. Play by the rules and demand the same from your opponent. You can, for example, insist on the measurement of questionable shoes without being a poor sport. Your opponent will not be offended by your attempt to benefit from rules, but he or she will be offended if you try to stretch or skirt rules, especially if it's an attempt to hurt his or her performance.

10. Dress appropriately. The dress code for horseshoe pitchers is loose. Jeans and shorts are acceptable. Shoes should have a firm sole that prevents the foot from turning over. Don't lose sight of your two main clothing goals: comfort and lack of distraction. The advantage of having regular pitching clothes is that you won't be conscious of your appearance when you compete, eliminating one more possible distraction. Many players wear shirts with their name and club or home town on the back.

The following are the stories of some horseshoe pitchers who pursued excellence.

Dave Loucks started pitching horseshoes back when he was still called "Davie." While living in San Francisco, he entered a citywide tournament for juniors. "I was twelve and looking for something to do, another activity," he remembers. "I picked up some old shoes and threw a flip turn. A veteran pitcher named Luke Braun took me under his wing and showed me how to hold the shoe, how to make it turn one and a quarter times." Dave must have been a quick study—he won the city championship for pitchers, age twelve and under.

The next year, Loucks came back in the thirteen-to-fifteen class and won another city championship. The local horseshoe pooh-bahs shooed him onto a bus bound for Murray, Utah, where he promptly won the Junior Boys World Championship, going 15–0. He repeated as champion in '52 and '53.

"Apparently, I had an innate ability in this area," Loucks understates.

Back in the fifties, the rules prohibited sixteen-year-olds from competing as juniors—they were considered adults. So when Dave turned sixteen, he faced a difficult choice: Pitch with the adults and jeopardize his amateur status (he was a promising baseball player) or give up horseshoes. He gave up horseshoes, commencing a retirement from tournaments that lasted six years.

Returning to the game in the service, he twice won the Twelfth Naval Championship. "Admiral Nimitz was an avid pitcher," Dave recalls. "He'd send his aide for me and we'd pitch together. I wasn't sure about the etiquette, so I usually let him win."

Out of the Navy and raising a family, Loucks went through another fallow period. For ten years he pitched only occasionally. Then in the mid-seventies, his kids nearly grown, he returned to the game he loved.

More than forty years after he began, Loucks has accumulated some impressive credentials. He maintained at least a 60 percent ringer average for twenty years, won three world titles, threw a 90 percent game (and lost), all of which earned him induction into the Horseshoe Pitchers Hall of Fame.

Yet his greatest contribution to the sport has probably been administrative. It began quite by accident. Back in the mid-eighties, his Pleasanton, California group bid for the World Tournament. "The previous high purse for a horseshoes tournament had been $20,000," he says, "and I came in promising $40,000. Apparently, the national organization didn't believe we could do it, because they awarded the tournament to a city in Wisconsin.

Then, an hour later, they voted me in as president and said, 'Now make it work.' That was more than ten years ago. Pleasanton got the tournament in 1988, and our prize money is now up over $100,000."

Loucks is proud of what he sees as a rejuvenation of the NHPA during his presidency. When his stewardship began, the average age of association members was sixty-something; today, it's fifty-two (and even lower if you don't count retired members). "We do what we can to attract juniors, what with scholarship funds and all," he says, "but we have an unfortunate image to overcome, that of the old-timers in bib overalls out pitching behind the barn."

Bonnie Robbins, fourteen, was bitten by the horseshoe bug when she was nine. She accompanied her horseshoe-pitching dad to the state tournament, where some junior-girl pitchers caught her eye. "Everyone seemed to be friends with everybody else," she remembers. "I'm a very social person, and they looked like they were having fun. I told my dad if they can play, I can play. He got me some shoes, took me to a little stump in the ground, and told me to throw at the stump. I was making ringers and feeling good. Dad told me I could join a club and pitch regularly, so long as I took it seriously. I decided to do it. At first it was tough. I had to throw a hundred shoes to get my average. I started out at zero-point-zero."

Now four years later, she is a gangly teenager who carries a 30 percent average and wins most of her games. In 1994 she won the California Junior Girls Championship. "Yeah, here I am fourteen, and I'm going to defend my championship," she says with a toothy grin. "I'm glad I stuck with it. If I hadn't, I'd be mad at myself for being a quitter."

Like so many juniors, she throws a flip. "I started out throwing a turn, but it didn't work for me," she says. "Dad said to throw whatever was comfortable, so I switched."

Although Bonnie has grooved a swing, her dominant strength may be mental toughness. "The mental skills are more important than the physical ones," she says, sounding unnervingly mature. "You can't be concentrating on what you're doing tomorrow and throw horseshoes. You've got to be concentrating on what you're doing now, on the shoe getting to the stake. Once you figure out the mental part of the game, you figure out how to throw the shoe right. And when you throw the shoe right, everything works."

Russ Peterich's earliest horseshoes recollections are right out of a Norman Rockwell painting. "I was ten, living in a little farming town," he says. "We'd have family meals, and my grandad, dad, and uncle would always pitch horseshoes after dinner. It was just two stakes driven in the ground, nothing fancy, but fun."

As a grown-up, Peterich lost track of the game for several years. Every year at the county fair he would linger at the horseshoe tournament, but only as a spectator. A high-school teacher and baseball coach, he already had his hands full.

After horseshoe courts were built in the park where his baseball team played, he would wander over to watch the local pitchers. One day he asked a veteran pitcher what it took to get involved.

"Nothing to it," the man replied. "Just get some shoes, come on out, and we'll teach you how to throw."

"Where do you get shoes?" Peterich asked.

"Well, y'know, I happen to have an extra pair in the trunk of my car. You can borrow 'em."

Once they got the shoes, Peterich had another question.

"How do you throw them?"

"Just grab and throw."

Lacking more precise guidelines, Peterich threw a flip. Four years later, he is an avid pitcher with a solid one-and-one-quarter turn. He finished last season with a 43 percent ringer average. That pales compared to the 80-plus percentages that dominate the World Tournament, but it is no small feat after only three years. Now he is trying to master the one-and-three-quarters turn, which he believes holds even more promise. He has taken a step backward with the hope of one day taking two steps forward. Out of such risk springs excellence, he believes, or at least progress.

"This is a great game," Peterich suddenly enthuses, like a kid at the fair. "It's like bowling, except bowling is easier because the ball is on the ground quickly, where it's easier to control. Here it's all through the air. Timing and judgment of distance are so critical in horseshoes. So is consistency and concentration. There are plenty of distractions." He gestures toward the serried rows of courts, where forty matches are in progress. "It's a great game.

One time I was just about to pitch, when a guy on the next court rung my ankle. I looked down and the horseshoe was just hanging around my ankle like I was a stake. We laughed about it, but then I had to be able to get back to business."

Why does a man in his fifties, with a family, his own baseball team, and a full life, take up shoes? "The best thing about horseshoes is the people you meet," Peterich answers unhesitatingly. His gaze sweeps over the sea of pitchers. "These are quality people. The ultimate sportsmen. You don't see people here getting upset or arguing calls like you do in baseball. You make a couple of ringers and your opponent will probably say, 'Those are great shoes.' The game always begins and ends with a handshake, something you don't find too often in competition."

Gail Sluys was about eighteen the first time she ever pitched horseshoes. She was living with her parents in New Jersey, and her aunt and uncle lived next door. Her dad and uncle put up a horseshoes court in between the two houses. "Once in a while, they let me play," she says. "I didn't know anything about it, but I loved it, even though they made me throw from forty feet."

After she was married, she and husband Casey would sometimes pound in a couple of stakes on a camping trip. But horseshoes remained a decidedly casual pursuit for the Sluys family until Casey developed the pitching passion and joined a local club. "He invited me to go with him," she says. "He promised to teach me how to keep score, so I said okay."

Gail made a point of trying to keep score for the best available pitchers. She would study their style and technique, until one day she heard a little voice say, "You could do that."

"I started pitching at 13 percent," she recalls. "Back then, they threw all the women into one group, so I was throwing against some 70 percent pitchers. Part of me thought, 'What am I doing here?' Another part of me wanted to become as good as they were."

Her more daring, ambitious side won out. She stayed with the game—and improved. "My goal each year was the next percentage level. The second year I wanted 20 percent; the third year 30 percent. Above 60 percent is an 'A' pitcher, and that's what I was aiming for. When I wasn't pitching, I did a lot of watching, a lot of scorekeeping."

Her confidence continued to swell, along with her ringer average, which topped 70 percent in 1994. "My goals continue to rise," she says. "Now I want to win the state title. I finished third last year. After that, I want to win the World."

Gail, presently ranked twenty-sixth in the world, doesn't see her main obstacles as physical. "The game takes coordination and stamina," she says, "but I lost the state last year because my concentration fell apart. The mental aspect of the game is definitely more important. If you have the mental part, you can get the physical part."

Gail believes the difference in mental tenacity between great and not-so-great pitchers is evident even to the casual observer. "If you watch the top levels, you notice that there's very little talk. As you drop down in class, there's more and more chatter. That's why they're not pitching as well. Many have the physical ability, but they won't take the next step up.

"My advice to the beginner who wants to move up: Practice and be quiet."

Casey Sluys never played horseshoes as a kid. He got his first taste when he was twenty-four and engaged to Gail. He played backyard horseshoes a few times with Gail's dad and uncle, then lost track of the sport for several years.

In the mid-eighties, Casey saw a newspaper ad for an amateur horseshoe pitching tournament. Although he had never thrown anything but a backyard shoe, some ineffable force pushed him to enter the tournament.

"Maybe it was that I was just old enough to be tired of all the sprained ankles in baseball," he says. "Anyway, I ended up placing second, my first trophy for anything. Spurred by that little success and by the nice people I'd met, I joined the local association. Later, I became secretary-treasurer, then president, then second vice president of the national association."

Sluys's ringer percentage climbed steadily from 6 percent, to 12 percent, to 18 percent, eventually peaking last year at 43 percent. "I definitely feel that administration hurts my concentration," he says. "Now that I'm a vice president with the national association, I hear every little comment or criticism by spectators. I carry a pad and pencil and take notes. It's my job to address those things later, but it doesn't make me a better pitcher."

What does help? Casey suggests starting early and getting in touch with a local club. (Check "Resources" or contact the NHPA for the club nearest you.) "Enter a tournament, learn to handle a little pressure. The horseshoe experience tends to be a positive one. There's a lot of patting on the back."

HALL OF FAMERS

Ted Allen was the sport's first real superstar. Born in 1908, he has been called, among other superlatives, "the best horseshoe pitcher who ever lived" and "the Babe Ruth of the sport." Allen played in thirty-one world tournaments between 1933 and 1973, winning the championship a record ten times. He holds numerous World Tournament records: 771 total victories; 72 consecutive ringers; a qualifying round in which he amassed 187 ringers out of 200 shoes; 12 consecutive four-deads; a 174-shoe game with Curt Day in 1957 in which the two combined for 155 ringers, 55 four-deads, 69 doubles, and an 89 percent ringer average.

Allen, an inveterate ambassador for the sport, liked to say he spent "forty years on the road," barnstorming all over the United States, Canada, and Cuba, pitching exhibitions at rodeos, theaters, sporting events, even doing a stint with the Barnum and Bailey circus. In all, he entertained and educated the masses from small towns to Madison Square Garden.

"I had to make a living, and horseshoe pitching was my life," he said.

Curt Day, who threw a three-quarters reverse turn from a crossfire position, was three times world champion and eighteen times Indiana state champion. In 17 appearances in the championship division of the world tournament, he won 495 and lost 83, with a ringer average above 80 percent. In 149 tournaments between 1960 and 1976, he hit 80 percent in 130 of them.

Harry "Pop" Woodfield was an acrobat, boxer, and horseshoe-pitching promoter. As NHPA president (1941–48), he contacted President Harry Truman, a well-known pitching aficionado, and helped install a court at the White House. He presented an NHPA membership card to Truman.

Dan and Sue Kuchcinski, husband and wife, each won three world championships, but they reached a far wider audience when they created an act that combined trick horseshoe pitching and acrobatics. Billed as "Mr. and Mrs. Horseshoes," they toured the United States, Canada, and Japan, playing to audiences that ranged from appreciative to awe-stricken.

As an audience warmup, Sue, a former Indiana state gymnastics champion, would do a straddle split right in front of the stake and Dan would pitch over her head and onto the stake. Even more jaw-dropping was the routine in which Sue stood on two chairs, did a backbend, and rested her head on the stake— while Dan tossed ringers. The record suggests that when Dan missed, he missed short.

The Kuchcinskis performed their act on the *Mike Douglas Show,* the *Merv Griffin Show, What's My Line,* and *To Tell the Truth.* But horseshoe pitching no doubt received its greatest exposure on April 16, 1968, when Dan and Sue's son, nineteen-year-old Danny Kuchcinski, appeared on the *Tonight Show* with Johnny Carson. An estimated 30 million viewers watched Kuchcinski put on an impressive exhibition of trick pitching. Carson, whose confidence was no doubt bolstered by Dan's résumé, which included his sixty-six straight ringers, played along by placing his chin on a stake while the 1967 world champion fired a ringer on his second try. Then Carson straddled the stake, positioning himself with one foot on each side of the horseshoe box, his crotch directly over the stake. He drew the expected ribbing from Ed McMahon, who pointed out the anatomical consequences of a Kuchcinski miss.

Horseshoe pitching has long been a family affair, and there have been some prolific families.

The American Directory of Horseshoe Pitching, a who's who of the sport, lists six Kuchcinskis and thirteen Renos, which begs the question of whether heredity or environment is the greater influence. Put the two together and the alchemy can produce some impressive results.

Consider the unsurpassed excellence of the family of Esther and Walter Ray Williams, Sr. Husband, wife, and all seven children (four boys, three girls) have been champion horseshoe pitchers. Walter Ray, Sr., who has been secretary-treasurer and vice president of NHPA, has pitched and promoted horseshoes since 1959. He has organized clubs and directed tournaments. Yet he is, as his son Jeff Williams points out, "the only member of the family not to win a state title."

Jeff Williams, who was the 1988 world champion, spoke to me about his particular branch of the family tree. As he talked, he repeatedly took draws on a beer, apparently a between-games ritual for him. "I started playing in tournaments in 1969, when I was eight and a half," he said. "The family always played tournaments, never barnyard horseshoes. In 1971, Walter Ray, Jr., who's a year older, won the World Junior Championship. At eleven, he was the youngest world champion ever. In 1972 he repeated, throwing forty straight ringers at one point. Then in 1973, I won it. Walter Ray hurt his hand that year but competed anyway and finished fourth. That same year, littlest brother Nathan was on the Charles Kuralt program for horseshoe excellence. He was six."

Although Jeff went on to repeat as junior champion in 1976 and to win the Class A World Championship in 1988 and 1989, it is six-time world champion Walter Ray who has shined the brightest.

When Jeff is asked what the biggest difference is between his play and Walter Ray's, he answers, "My brother is out there to win and be perfect. I'm out there for relaxation and fun. . . . " Just then, a knowledgeable bystander motions toward the can of beer in Jeff's hand and says, "That's the difference between Jeff and Walter Ray." Jeff seems to take this potential insult in stride. He smiles and says matter-of-factly, "Walter Ray's got a killer instinct, and that's what it takes to win the game."

Jeff admits that diligent practice has made his brother what he is today. "At his peak, Walter Ray practiced two hours a day every day. At my peak, I practiced two hours a day, three times a week. Practice is important. It takes so long to get to the top class, usually at least five years (though Walter Ray made it in six months). They say close only counts in horseshoes, but not at the top level. Ringers count. You miss a ringer and it hurts."

It seems that everyone has a Walter Ray story. Jerry Smith, who runs tournaments out of Davis, California, recalls that

Former world champion Harold Reno offers ten hints for getting better:

1. Get plenty of sleep, good food, and exercise, and avoid bad habits that hurt your health.
2. Pick out a spot to stand every time.
3. Set no goals, except to do your best.
4. Find a way to relax before you pitch each shoe. I do it by an extra swing of my arms, but other pitchers do it other ways.
5. Don't change anything without a good reason or without giving it a good chance. If you are improving with your turn, with your brand of shoe, with your stance, don't go to another.
6. Try to practice some every day. I cannot find time to do this myself, but I would recommend that you pitch one hundred or more shoes each day.
7. Blot out interference. Don't talk to people, listen to noises, or watch something going on outside the courts while you play.
8. Pitch one shoe at a time and play one game at a time. Worrying about percentages or about upcoming opponents can lessen your concentration.
9. Try to get an early lead. This will put the pressure on your opponent and give you confidence.
10. Be a good sport.

before the 1989 state tournament, Walter Ray rolled into town to play in a little pretournament tournament that Jerry was throwing. "Walter Ray looked at the competition, saw there wasn't anyone above fifty percent, and asked if he could pitch left-handed. I said yes, except that he would have to use his right-handed average for handicap purposes. He said he didn't care about that.

"So he threw left-handed and his first game was sixty-five

percent. He finished the day at fifty-five percent." Jerry paused and dabbed at his eye—it was easy to imagine him wiping away a tear. "I'm a left-handed pitcher," he added, "and that made me feel real bad."

Another pitcher with a Williams story, though it's questionable how often he tells it, is Richard Pintor of Colorado. In 1988 he lost to Walter 40–0 and to his brother Nathan 45–1.

RULES

....

Official Rules of Horseshoe Pitching
as published by the
National Horseshoe Pitchers Association of America

RULE 1: COURT LAYOUT (SEE FIGURES 1–4)

Section A: Permanent Ground-Level Courts

1. Dimensions. A horseshoe court shall be a level rectangular area 6 feet wide and a minimum of 46 feet long. A north-south setting is recommended for outdoor courts to minimize the effects of the sun.
2. Pitcher's Box. The pitcher's box is the 6-foot by 6-foot square area at each end of the court. It is composed of two parts, the pits and the pitching platforms.

    a. Pit. The pit is a rectangular area filled with the substance onto which the shoes are pitched. Its maximum length (the direction the shoes are pitched) is 72 inches; its minimum length is 43 inches. Maximum width is 36 inches; minimum width is 31 inches. The pit must be centered in the pitcher's box. If the pit is less than the maximum dimensions, the extra space shall be filled with the same material of which the platforms are made, or some other material different than the pit substance, and shall be level with the pit and platforms.

    b. Pitching Platforms. The pitching platforms flank the pit on both its left and right side, parallel to each other. They shall be level with each other and to the top of the pit. They shall be 18 to $20\frac{1}{2}$ inches wide, depending on the width of the pit, and shall be a minimum of 6 feet long.
3. Stakes. The stake is the target at which the shoe is pitched. Normally, the fronts of the stakes are 40 feet apart. Each stake shall be centered between the platforms, with a minimum of 21 inches from the stake to both the front and back of the pit. Stakes shall be 1 inch in diameter and may be

made of cold-rolled steel, mild iron, soft metal, or synthetic material. Each stake shall be no shorter than 14 inches and no higher than 15 inches above pit level, and they shall both have an approximate 3-inch lean toward each other.

4. Pit Substance. Clay, sand, dirt, and synthetic compositions are all legal substances to put in the pit. The minimum depth of the substance shall be 4 inches. An 8-inch depth is recommended.

5. Extended Platforms. The pitching platforms on either side of the pit shall be extended forward (toward the opposite pit) an additional 10 feet to accommodate pitching at shorter distances. The front of the extended platforms shall be 27 feet from the opposite stake. The extended platforms shall be level with and be of the same width and material as the full-distance platforms. It is recommended that the 14 feet between the front ends of the platforms be filled in, using the same material as the platforms, to provide a continuous level walking surface between the two pitchers' boxes.

6. Multiple Courts

   a. Side-by-Side. To eliminate distraction and safely separate activity, stakes of courts adjacent to each other shall be a minimum of 10 feet apart—12 feet is preferable.

   b. Back-to-Back. A minimum of 16 feet and a protective barrier must separate the stakes of back-to-back courts.

7. Backboards and Protective Barrier

   a. Backboards. Every pit should have a backboard. It should be at least 4 feet behind the stake, be at least 1 foot high, and extend the width of the pit. For spectator visibility, a mesh netting or chain-link material is recommended. If of solid material, it should be a color that will provide a contrasting background so as to keep the stake visible to the contestants.

   b. Protective Barrier. All court complexes shall be surrounded by a protective barrier. The barrier should be at least 8 feet behind the stake. A chain-link-type fence at least 4 feet high is recommended.

8. Foul Lines. Foul lines shall be defined by lines extending across the front of the full-distance and extended platforms. This places them 37 feet and 27 feet respectively from the opposite stakes. They shall be level with the platforms and marked so that any contact with a line will constitute a foul.

9. Imaginary Stakes. Imaginary stakes shall be marked midway between the left and right extended platforms at a distance of 30 feet from the opposite stakes. They shall also be marked on the full-distance platforms at a distance of 40 feet from the opposite stakes if the stakes are not 40 feet apart.

Section B: Covered and Indoor Courts

The regulations for covered and indoor courts are exactly the same as for permanent ground-level courts, with the added stipulation that they shall have a minimum 12-foot vertical clearance to the lowest possible obstruction.

Section C: Temporary and/or Raised Courts

The regulations for temporary and/or raised courts are the same as for permanent ground-level courts, with the exception that for any raised court, the top of the pit shall be no more than 7 inches above the level of the pitching platforms. In addition, the 4-inch pit substance requirement is recommended, but not mandatory.

Note: The NHPA realizes that many sets of courts now in existence do not meet all of the conditions listed in Rule 1. All new courts shall be constructed using the guidelines in Rule 1, and charters are encouraged to modify their existing courts to meet these standards as soon as possible.

RULE 2: PLAYING EQUIPMENT—THE HORSESHOE

Section A: Legal Shoes

The sport of horseshoes is played with specially manufactured equipment. Any official (legal) horseshoe must be sanctioned and approved by the NHPA and must pass the following maximum weight and measurement standards (there are no minimum standards): 1. it shall not weigh more than 2 pounds, 10 ounces; 2. it shall not exceed $7^{1}/_{4}$ inches in width, and $7^{5}/_{8}$ inches in length, and the opening of the shoe must not exceed $3^{1}/_{2}$ inches. A $^{1}/_{8}$-inch tolerance to $3^{5}/_{8}$ inches is allowed on used shoes. Shoes not meeting these requirements shall not be used in NHPA-sanctioned competition, and all games pitched with illegal shoes shall be forfeited.

Section B: Altered Shoes

Any shoe that has been changed from its original design (calk, notch, etc.) shall be considered an "altered" shoe. An altered shoe is illegal and cannot be used in sanctioned play.

Note: The NHPA Executive Council has the right to waive the altered shoe provision for a physically impaired contestant.

Section C: Shoes Sanctioned by Other Countries

Any shoes sanctioned by another country are permissible in NHPA sanctioned play only for contestants from that country, and then only if they meet NHPA specifications. They are not allowable for U.S. citizens for NHPA-sanctioned events unless they are also sanctioned by the NHPA.

RULE 3: PITCHING DISTANCES

Section A: Males

1. Juniors. Junior contestants may pitch from any place on either the full-distance or extended platforms. They must observe the 27-foot foul lines.
2. Open Men's and Seniors. All open men's and senior contestants shall pitch from on or behind the full-distance platforms adjacent to the pits and observe the 37-foot foul lines.

   Physically impaired males in these categories may be given permission by the governing NHPA officials to move onto the extended platforms and observe the 27-foot foul lines.
3. Elders. Elders, classified as short-distance pitchers, shall pitch less than the full distance and observe the 27-foot foul lines.

Section B: Females

All female contestants may pitch from any place on the full distance or extended platforms and observe the 27-foot foul lines, except that any woman pitching in an elders class must pitch less than 40 feet.

RULE 4: PIT PREPARATION AND MAINTENANCE

Section A
Every effort shall be made to keep the substance in the pit in soft, puttylike condition so the shoes do not bounce or move around after coming in contact with the substance. If necessary, the substance in the pit shall be watered and leveled to the top of the surrounding platforms (unless the pits are raised) before a game starts. Each contestant is responsible for one pit, but a contestant may have someone else do the preparation. During a game, a contestant shall not step on, mash, or otherwise repair any of the substance in the scoring area of the pit without the consent of the opponent or a tournament official. Repair needed because of a measured shoe or a "buried" shoe shall be handled using the same guidelines.

Note: Pits composed of sand or dirt often "hollow out" after a few innings. A blanket statement by the tournament director (made before competition begins) shall allow the leveling of these courts as needed without constant consent between the contestants.

Section B
With the permission of the tournament committee, the stakes may be painted for visibility purposes before a game starts. This procedure shall not be done while a game is in progress, unless both contestants agree to do it.

RULE 5: GAME PREPARATION

It is customary for contestants to find out their court assignments and warm up on that court for their first game with the proper opponent. The court should be prepared for play during this time. When the tournament official announces the start of play, the contestants shall flip a shoe or coin, with the winner having the choice of first or second pitch.

After a game is completed, a contestant shall go to the next assigned court and prepare one pit for play. When the other contestant arrives, the same procedure shall be followed. When both contestants have arrived and prepared the pits, they may pitch four warm-up shoes each and then must start their game, using the method described in the previous paragraph to decide first pitch. It is legal for a contestant to practice alone if the second contestant is late in arriving.

RULE 6: PLAY OF THE GAME AND VALUE OF THE SHOE

Section A: Innings
The game is broken down into innings. Each inning consists of four pitched shoes, two by each contestant.

Section B: Value of the Shoe
1. Ringer. A ringer is a shoe that comes to rest encircling the stake. A straightedge touching both points of the shoe must clear (not touch) the stake in order for a shoe to be declared a ringer. A ringer has a value of three points.
2. Shoe in Count. A shoe that is not a ringer but comes to rest with any portion of it within 6 inches of any part of the stake is a shoe in count. A shoe in count has a value of one point. A "leaner," or any other shoe touching the stake (but not a ringer), is considered a shoe in count and has a value of one point.
3. Shoe out of Count. A shoe that comes to rest farther than 6 inches from the stake is a shoe out of count and has no scoring value. A shoe that is declared a foul shoe (see Section H) is considered a shoe out of count, no matter where it comes to rest.

Section C: Delivery of Shoes
1. The contestant pitching first shall deliver both shoes one at a time, and then the other contestant shall deliver both shoes one at a time. A contestant may deliver the shoes from either the left or right platform, but in any one inning both shoes must be delivered from the same platform. If both contestants use the same platform to deliver their shoes, the contestant pitching first (after delivering both shoes) should cross over to the other side in front of the pit and then move to the rear of that platform. As the first contestant is crossing over in front, the second contestant should be crossing over in back and mounting the platform from the rear.

2. A contestant shall deliver both shoes within thirty seconds. The time shall start for the first contestant when the pitching platform is taken in preparation to pitch, after both contestants have retrieved their shoes. The time shall start for the second contestant upon taking the platform after the first contestant has delivered the two shoes.

   Note: Extra time taken to repair a damaged shoe by filing a burr, or a delay resulting from a distraction not caused by a contestant, shall not be penalized.

Section D: Position of Contestants during Delivery

1. The Pitcher. During the entire address and delivery of a shoe, when a contestant's foot is in contact with the ground, it must be in contact with the designated pitching platform. The lone exception is that the contestant may stand behind (but not to the side of) the full-distance platform. No contact either on or over the foul line is allowed until after the shoe is released.

2. The Opponent. The opponent, while not pitching, shall stand on or behind the other platform, at least 2 feet to the rear of the contestant who is pitching. If the competition is mixed (in terms of pitching distances), the opponent shall move to the rear of the full-distance platform. The opponent shall be quiet and stationary so as not to disturb the contestant who is pitching or contestants on adjacent courts.

3. No contestant shall walk to the opposite stake (except to remove a foul shoe) or be informed of the position of any pitched shoes prior to the completion of an inning.

Section E: Flow of the Game

1. Once the four shoes of an inning have been pitched, the contestants shall walk to the other end to determine the score for the inning and retrieve their shoes. No shoe shall be moved before its scoring value is determined. If the decision is in doubt, a judge shall be called. The judge shall make the necessary measurements and determine the scoring for the shoes in question.

   Contestants are encouraged to carry measuring devices and make their own decisions whenever possible to help speed up play. Play shall continue in similar fashion in each inning until the game limit is reached.

2. At any one time, a contestant shall carry and use only two horseshoes during the course of a game. A spare shoe or shoes should be kept available at courtside in case of a broken shoe or if the contestant desires to switch shoes. Shoes may be switched between innings, but not during an inning unless a shoe breaks (see Section F).

3. If it is discovered during an inning that a contestant has pitched the shoe of an opponent, the shoes shall be picked up and the entire inning shall be repitched using the correct shoes. If the contestants fail to discover the error until after all four shoes have been pitched, the inning shall be scored on the basis of whatever shoes they pitched. If agreement cannot be reached, a judge shall be called. Based upon input from the contestants, the judge shall either determine the scoring for the inning or void it and order it repitched.

4. When a shoe is being measured by a contestant and it (or the stake) is accidentally moved, the inning shall be scored only if the contestants can come to an agreement. If no agreement can be reached, a judge shall be called. As in item 3 above, the judge shall either determine the scoring or void the inning and order it repitched.

    Note: If a judge moves a shoe (or a stake) while making a measurement, the judge shall either determine the scoring for the inning or void it and order it repitched.

5. It is legal for contestants to use a hook or similar device to retrieve the shoes. Care should be taken in using the hook, so as not to endanger the opponent. Also, contestants are encouraged to carry a file and towel to keep their horseshoes smooth and shoes and hands clean and dry.

Section F: Broken and Cracked Shoes

1. Broken Shoes

    a. If a shoe breaks into two or more parts when it hits the stake or lands in the pit, the parts shall be removed and another shoe shall be allowed to be pitched in its stead. If the shoe breaks when striking the backboard or other "foul" ground, it is foul and may not be repitched.

    b. If a shoe has landed in the pit and becomes broken by having another shoe land on it, it shall be scored as it appears to lay. If there is any disagreement, a judge shall be called. The judge shall either determine the scoring for the inning or void it and order it repitched.

2. Cracked Shoes. If a shoe is discovered to be cracked (but not completely broken in two), it shall be scored as it lays.

Section G: Broken Stakes

A broken stake is defined as any stake not in the same position as when the game started, and which both contestants agree is broken. When a stake breaks during an inning, the game shall be discontinued at the end of the previous inning and the stake replaced. If a stake breaks as a result of being struck by the fourth shoe of the inning and both contestants agree as to the results of the inning, then it shall be counted. If they cannot agree, then a judge shall be called. The judge shall either determine the scoring for the inning or void it and order it repitched. Once the scoring is determined, the tournament officials may decide to complete the game on another court or hold the completion until a later time. Once the stake is replaced, the contestants may take four warm-up shoes each, if they so desire, and then play shall resume.

Section H: Foul Shoe

A foul shoe is a shoe that was delivered in noncompliance with one of the rules of the game. Considered a shoe out of count, it is to be removed from the pit (if it is within the scoring radius of the stake), before any more shoes are pitched. Shoes already in the pit that have been disturbed by a foul shoe are not to be moved. They shall remain as they lay.

1. The following are rule violations that must be spotted and called by an assigned judge. The penalty is to declare the shoe a foul shoe.

a. Any shoe pitched when the contestant has stepped on or over the foul line.

b. Any shoe pitched when a contestant's foot has not been in contact with the pitcher's platform. Exception: The foot may be behind the platform with no penalty.

c. Any shoe not delivered within the thirty-second time limit.

d. Any shoe pitched when a contestant illegally steps on the scoring area of the playing surface. When this violation occurs, the contestant shall pitch only one shoe in the next inning. The second shoe shall be carried to the other end.

e. The second shoe, if it is pitched from a different platform than the first shoe.

2. The following occurrences are also considered foul shoes, and the shoes must be removed from the pit (if they are within the scoring radius of the stake) before any more shoes are delivered.

a. Any shoe that contacts the background, court frame, or any ground outside the pit before it comes to rest.

b. Any shoe that strikes a previously defined object, such as a tree limb, wire, or indoor court ceiling.

Note: A shoe that strikes a moving foreign object is not a foul shoe and may be repitched.

c. The second shoe, if the contestant changes shoes after the first shoe has been pitched. The only exception is if a first shoe has broken in two and qualifies for a repitch.

d. Count any shoe that leaves a contestant's hand once the final forward swing of the delivery has started. If it touches any ground outside of the target pit, it shall be counted as a foul shoe. A shoe that is accidentally dropped by a contestant before the final forward swing has started shall not be considered foul and may be picked up and pitched.

3. A contestant's shoes shall be called foul if the contestant removes any shoe before the scoring of that shoe has been agreed upon. A judge shall be called if a decision cannot be reached. The judge shall determine the scoring for the inning.

Section I: Protests

If a contestant desires to make a protest, the protest shall be made to the judge or tournament official at the time the problem occurs. The tournament committee shall make the final ruling on all protests.

RULE 7: LENGTH OF GAME

The length of a game shall be determined before play begins. There are two options:

1. Point Limit. The game shall be played to a predetermined number of points. The first contestant to reach (or exceed) that amount is the winner.
2. Shoe Limit. The game shall be played to a predetermined number of shoes. It shall be an even number. When that amount is reached, the contestant with the highest score is the winner. If the score is tied, there are two options:

    a. Each contestant shall receive one-half win and one-half loss. This option should be used if a handicap system is in effect.

    b. A two-inning tiebreaker shall be played, using the same method of play that was used in the game. In the event of another tie, the same process shall be repeated, and this procedure shall continue until the tie is broken.

RULE 8: SCORING THE GAME, SINGLES PLAY

There are two methods of scoring in horseshoes—cancellation and count-all.

Section A: Cancellation Scoring

1. Basic Scoring. In cancellation scoring, only one contestant can score in each inning.

    a. Ringers. Ringers cancel each other out. A ringer of one contestant shall cancel the ringer of the other contestant, and those shoes shall not score any points. Any uncanceled (live) ringer scores three points.

    b. Shoes in Count. A shoe in count shall score one point under the following conditions:

    1) If there are canceled ringers and no live ringer, the closest shoe in count to the stake shall score one point.

    2) If there are no ringers, the closest shoe in count shall score one point. If the other shoe of that same contestant is the second closest shoe in count, it shall also score one point.

    3) If there is one uncanceled ringer and the other shoe of the scoring contestant is the closest shoe in count to the stake, it shall score one point (four points total).

    Note: Opposing contestant's shoes in count that are touching the stake or are determined to be an equal distance from the stake shall cancel each other and, like cancelled ringers, shall score no points. In that situation, the next closest shoe in count, if there is one, shall score one point.

2. Calling the Score.

a. Points shall be awarded in the following situations. The contestant scoring the points shall call the score.

1) No ringer with the closest shoe in count—call "one point."

2) No ringer with the two closest shoes in count—call "two points."

3) One ringer with either no shoe in count or the other contestant having the closest shoe in count—call "one ringer, three points."

4) One ringer with the closest shoe in count—call "one ringer, four points."

5) Two canceled ringers with the closest shoe in count—call "one ringer each, one point."

6) Two canceled ringers with one uncanceled ringer—call "three ringers, three points.

7) Two uncanceled ringers—call "two ringers, six points."

b. No points shall be awarded in the following situations. The score shall be called by the contestant who pitched second.

1) All four shoes out of count—call "no score."

2) Two canceled ringers with no shoes in count or with the other two shoes an equal distance from the stake—call "one ringer each, no score."

3) Four canceled ringers—call "four dead."

Section B: Count-All Scoring

In count-all scoring, both contestants receive credit for the number of points their own shoes are worth in each inning. Because both contestants can score in the same inning (each contestant can score zero, one, two, three, four, or six points in each inning), care should be taken in reporting the scores to the scorekeeper so that the proper score is recorded for each contestant.

Section C: Recording the Score.

In tournament play, the score sheet (not the scoring device) shall be the official record of the game. Contestants are encouraged to pay close attention to the score at all times. If a question or discrepancy occurs regarding the correct score, the contestants may approach the scorer between innings or during their half-inning to rectify the situation. If the discrepancy cannot be corrected to the satisfaction of both contestants, a tournament judge shall be called to make the final decision.

RULE 9: PITCHING ROTATION DURING THE GAME

Section A: Cancellation Scoring

If the game is to be played under cancellation scoring, there are two ways to determine who shall pitch first in the next inning once the game has started. The method to be used shall be determined before play begins.

1. The contestant who scored in the preceding inning shall pitch first in the next inning. If neither pitcher scores, the contestant who pitched second (last) in the preceding inning shall pitch first in the next inning.

2. Alternate Pitch. Alternate first pitch is used to guarantee each contestant an equal amount of first and second pitches during a game. It can be done in three ways. If the game is to be played to a shoe limit, it is recommended that the limit be a number divisible by four.

    a. One contestant shall pitch first in innings one, four, five, eight, nine, twelve, thirteen, sixteen, seventeen, and so forth, and the other contestant shall pitch first in innings two, three, six, seven, ten, eleven, fourteen, fifteen, and so forth, until the game is completed. This is the fairest, and recommended, way.

    b. One contestant shall pitch first in innings one, two, five, six, nine, ten, thirteen, fourteen, and so on, while the other contestant shall pitch first in innings three, four, seven, eight, eleven, twelve, fifteen, sixteen, and so forth, until the game is completed.

    c. One contestant shall pitch first from one end and the opponent shall pitch first from the other end.

Section B: Count-all Scoring

Any game played using count-all scoring shall be played under an alternate pitch format found in A-2 above.

Section C: Handicap Scoring

Any game played under any kind of handicap system shall use an alternate pitch format.

Section D: Pitching out of Turn

If it is discovered during an inning (before all four shoes are pitched) that the wrong contestant has pitched first, the shoes pitched so far in that inning shall be picked up, and the inning shall be repitched. If the error is not discovered until after all four shoes have been delivered, they shall be scored as they lay, and the correct rotation shall be reestablished for the rest of the game.

RULE 10: DOUBLES PLAY

In doubles play, two contestants are partners against another team of two contestants. One contestant from each team shall be at each end of the court, and the contestants shall be matched by the tournament officials so that the highest-rated contestant (by percentage) from each team shall be at the same end. The tournament committee shall determine the length of game and type of play, and the scoring shall be done on one scoresheet, just as for singles play. When contestants are pitching their shoes, the contestants at the other end shall be well back and to the side of the pitcher's box (for their own safety) and in a stationary position so as not to disturb the contestants on their own and adjacent courts. Otherwise, all rules for singles play shall apply.

Section A: Regular Doubles

In regular doubles, each team uses one pair of shoes, and the contestants stay at the same end of the court for the entire game. To begin the game, the highest-rated contestants shall decide first pitch and pitch their shoes, just as in singles competition. Their partners at the other end shall decide and call the score, retrieve the shoes, and pitch them back, and the same procedure is followed. Who pitches first in each inning is determined by the scoring system being used, following the rules of singles play.

Section B: Walking Doubles

In walking doubles, all contestants shall use their own shoes. To begin the game, the highest-rated contestants shall decide first pitch and pitch their four shoes. The contestants at the opposite end shall then pitch their four shoes. After all eight shoes have been pitched, the contestants shall walk to the other end, decide the scoring, and retrieve their shoes. (An acceptable scoring alternative would have the contestants standing at the end to where the first pair of contestants pitched their shoes call the score of those shoes before they pitch.) Using one score sheet, the scores shall be recorded just as in a singles game, with the highest-rated contestants' scores recorded first each time. The same procedure shall then be repeated, with the highest-rated participants always going first. Who pitches first in each inning is determined by the scoring system being used, following the rules of singles play.

RULE 11: APPROPRIATE NHPA MEMBER CONDUCT

Section A: On the Courts

An NHPA member, while in competition, shall make no disturbing noises or movements that would distract the opponent or competitors on adjacent courts. A first offense shall call for a warning from the judge or tournament official. A second offense shall call for a forfeiture of the game being played. Any further offenses shall call for forfeiture of all games.

Section B: Unsportsmanlike Conduct

Any NHPA member who indulges in heckling, unfair rooting, or any other form of unsportsmanlike conduct toward any NHPA member or tournament official shall be subject to expulsion from the tournament and the tournament site. This covers any inappropriate behavior, including profane or abusive language, in or around the court area. The member shall also be subject to a one-year suspension from the NHPA.

RULE 12: TOURNAMENT PLAY

Section A: Type of Play
The standard method of NHPA-sanctioned tournament play is round-robin play with contestants being divided into classes. Each contestant will play every other contestant in the class.

Section B: Determining Winners
At the end of round-robin play, class winners shall be determined by win-loss records or ringer percentage. In addition, total points may be used if the scoring was done using the count-all method. If ties occur, they shall be settled by playoff, who beat whom, or one of the other methods that was not used to determine the winner. The tournament committee shall decide how winners are to be determined and how ties are to be broken, and announce these procedures before tournament play begins. If playoff games take place, the method of play and length of games shall be decided by the tournament committee.

Section C: Ringer Percentage
A contestant's ringer percentage shall be determined by dividing the total number of ringers by the total number of shoes pitched. Shoes pitched in playoff games and in extra innings that follow tie games shall be included in these totals.

Section D: Miscellaneous
The rules used to seed contestants in all NHPA-sanctioned tournaments are found in Articles X-XII of the NHPA bylaws. In addition, rules regarding game length, format, and tie-breaking situations in state, regional, national, and world championship play are found in the same articles. The NHPA dress code for World Tournament play is found in Article X. Its use is encouraged, but not required, for all NHPA-sanctioned play.

Section E: Handicapping
Handicapping may be used in open tournaments and league play. The amount of the handicap shall be determined by the tournament committee. Game handicapping shall not be used in any world, national, or regional tournament, or in the championship

class of a designated division of any state championship tournament.

RULE 13: TOURNAMENT ADMINISTRATION AND SANCTIONED LEAGUE ADMINISTRATION

Section A
All NHPA-sanctioned tournaments and leagues shall have a designated committee or director to administer the activities. The committee or director shall do the following:
1. Publicize the event.
   a. Announce the date, place, entry fee, prize list, registration deadline, and any other information a member will need in order to participate.
   b. Announce classifications available to entrants.
   c. Announce the method of play (cancellation or count-all), the length of the games (how many shoes or points), and whether or not alternate pitch will be used.
   d. Announce the method to be used for handling ties for individual games and at the end of round-robin play.
2. Obtain verifiable ringer percentages from NHPA charter statisticians (or NATSTATS) for all entrants.
3. Set up the playing format, assign contestants to their proper courts, and provide contestants with a schedule of games to be played.
4. Make sure all entrants are NHPA members.
5. Arrange for scorekeepers for each court and for their remuneration. The method and amount of pay shall be announced before play begins.
6. Have statisticians available for the compilation of tournament results.
7. Have judges available.
8. Handle all protests and make the final decisions on any items that come up.
9. Make the decision to halt play because of inclement weather and decide when play shall continue if conditions improve.
10. Make the awards and presentations at the end of play.
11. See that the results are sent to the charter statistician (and NATSTATS) for proper recording.

Section B: Judges

1. Judges shall be appointed by the tournament committee. Their duties are as follows:

    a. To enforce the rules and issue the proper penalties if violations occur.

    b. To measure for ringers, closest shoes to the stake, and shoes in count when asked to do so by contestants.

    c. To help make the proper decision in situations involving broken shoes, broken stakes, shoes and stakes moved by contestants during measurement, shoes pitched out of turn, and a contestant's shoes mistakenly pitched by an opponent.

    d. To act as liaison between the contestants and the tournament committee in all possible situations.

2. The decisions made by judges in 1 a-c above shall be accepted as final by the contestants, and the game shall resume from that point.

GLOSSARY

··

address: The alignment and aiming a pitcher does just before pitching.

alternate pitch: A way of deciding first and second pitch that assures each contestant an equal number of first and second pitches during a game.

calling the score: Communicating the score to the scorekeeper. The contestant scoring the points in the inning shall call the score.

cancellation scoring: A method of scoring in which like value cancels like value and only one contestant can score in each inning.

count-all scoring: A method of scoring in which all points are tallied and like value does not cancel like value. In this system, both players can score in the same inning.

elder: A competitive classification for pitchers seventy and over. Elders must observe the 27-foot foul line.

foul line: The line beyond which a pitcher may not go and still throw a legal shoe. For open men and seniors, the foul lines are 37 feet from the target stakes; for juniors, elders, and women, the foul lines are 27 feet from the target stakes.

foul shoe: A shoe pitched in violation of one or more rules. A foul shoe is a shoe out of count, no matter where it comes to rest.

four-dead: An inning in which all four shoes are ringers.

handicap: Predetermined number of bonus points given to a player in addition to the actual *(scratch)* score pitched in a game.

inning: Part of a game; two players have completed an inning when they have each thrown both of their shoes into the pit. A score is called and tallied at the completion of each inning.

junior: A competitive classification for youngsters age

seventeen and under. Juniors must observe the 27-foot foul lines.

leaner: A horseshoe that comes to rest leaning against the stake. In the olden days, leaners counted for more than just closest shoe, but no more.

National Horseshoe Pitchers Association of America (NHPA): The governing body of horseshoe pitching. It serves to promote, organize, and standardize various aspects of the sport.

percentage of handicap: System of compensating a lower-average player with a percentage (usually 80 or 90) of the difference between his handicap and his opponent's handicap.

pit: A rectangular area filled with the substance—usually clay—upon which the shoes are pitched. At its maximum, it should have a length of 72 inches and a width of 36 inches; at its minimum, it should be 43 inches long and 31 inches wide.

pitch: The act of delivering, in an underhand motion, a horseshoe toward a stake.

pitching platform: In an official court, the surfaces from which the pitchers pitch.

The pitching platforms, which flank both sides of the pit, are level with each other and with the top of the pit.

point limit: A predetermined number of points to which a game is played. The first contestant to reach or exceed that limit is the winner.

quoits: An ancient game in which a heavy, flattish ring of stone or metal was thrown as a test of strength or skill. The forerunner of modern horseshoes.

ringer: A shoe that encircles the stake so completely that a straightedge can be placed across the open end of the shoe, prong to prong, without touching the peg.

ringer average: The percentage of a pitcher's total throws that are ringers: the number of ringers divided by the number of throws.

senior: A competitive classification for pitchers age sixty and over. Senior men must observe the 37-foot foul line, while senior women observe the 27-foot foul line.

shoe in count: A shoe that is not a ringer but comes to rest with any part of it within 6 inches of any part of the stake. A shoe in count shall score one point if it is the closest shoe.

shoe limit: A predetermined number of shoes to be thrown in a game. When that shoe count is reached, the player with the highest score is the winner.

shoe out of count: A shoe that comes to rest farther than 6 inches from the stake and therefore has no scoring value. A foul shoe is a shoe out of count, regardless of where it comes to rest.

stake *(peg):* One of the two cold-rolled 1-inch-diameter steel rods that horseshoe pitchers aim for. Stakes should protrude 14 to 15 inches aboveground and be angled 3 inches toward the opposite stake.

RESOURCES

....

CLUBS

Suppose you want to become more seriously involved in horse-shoes. What do you do? Step one: Start hanging out with people who share your enthusiasm for the sport. In other words, join a club. To do so:

1. Start your own club. It might have a one- or two-family core, with neighbors or other family members joining as their interest grows.
2. Join an established club. This is typically an organized group of people who enjoy both the competitive and the social benefits of the game. They usually play on more formal, well-kept courts.
3. Join a country club or sports club that, although domi-nated by other sports, offers horseshoe pitching to its members.
4. Join a retirement community that has horseshoe pits.

To learn more about clubs, to update information, or to receive organizational assistance, contact the National Horseshoe Pitchers Association of America (NHPA) at 3085 76th St., Franksville, WI 53126, telephone and fax 414-835-9108.

The NHPA can also provide instructional materials, educa-tional clinics, tournament formats, equipment advice and dis-counts, and subscriptions to *Newsline,* the NHPA magazine. These benefits easily justify the annual dues.

The purpose of the NHPA is to foster, develop, and promote the sport of horseshoe pitching at all levels—local, state, regional, national, and international—both as a recreational pastime and as a competitive sport.

Any "reputable" person may become a member upon payment of annual dues (as of this writing, $12 for adults, $5 for juniors).

FORMATION OF LEAGUES

The NHPA fields lots of inquiries about starting and maintaining leagues. Many factors combine to determine how, or if, a club should run a league, including number and location of courts, lighting, number of pitchers, time available for pitching, and expected absenteeism because of work and vacations.

To be successful, a horseshoe club should have some type of weekly organized competition. The NHPA recommends a team league, with the teams playing a round-robin schedule of matches. Smaller groups can organize the competition around individual play, both singles and doubles, but larger clubs should create teams of three or more players. It is preferable to keep the number of players on each team small and have a larger number of teams.

The league schedule should be drawn up before the start of the season and all rules and provisions of play listed. Once rules and provisions are agreed upon, they should be adhered to, lest the league disintegrate into bickering.

The first set of rules may not cover all contingencies. It's best to establish an executive committee, composed of officers and team captains, who will rule on any disputes, or, alternatively, to empower one person to act as commissioner and make final decisions. Any such changes should eventually be incorporated into your league by-laws.

CLUB/LEAGUE RULES

Because of the variety of ways to set up leagues and clubs, it's impossible to write a sample constitution that all groups can use. Following are general topics that should be covered.

A. Officers and Their Duties. President, vice president, secretary, publicity director, statistician, executive committee, and activities committee to plan banquets, tournaments, court maintenance, and so forth.

B. Method of Play. Establish type of game (point limit or shoe limit), how many games per night, how many games per player, schedule of games, starting time, how long to wait before forfeit.

C. Playing Rules. Refer to the NHPA rules. Decide whether players will alternate first pitch. Alternating first pitch is highly recommended in handicap play. Post the rules prominently for all to see.

D. Postponements. Set time limit for the team captain to notify opposing captain if a game is to be postponed. Decide whether and when a rained-out match is to be played. Such a decision will depend on how rigid the schedule is for completion of the league.

E. Forfeits, Dummy Scores. Forfeits should, if possible, be avoided. If a player has no opponent, he may be required to pitch against a dummy score equal to his average or some set number of points. He must exceed that total to gain a win.

F. Handicaps. Decide method of handicapping (whether to use season average thus far or recent average, whether to use 100 percent, 90 percent, or 80 percent of handicap), and how often to change handicaps (usually weekly or biweekly).

G. Awards. Decide how many awards to give, what type they will be, and for what achievements they will be bestowed. Fix the minimum number of games to qualify for awards.

H. Dues. Determine the fixed amount to pitch in the league, and set a due date. Decide on extra charges for tournaments.

I. Sponsors. Solicit the help of local businesses to provide shirts, trophies, and so forth.

Be sure to have at least a trophy for the winning team's sponsor. Framed sponsor certificates are recommended.

J. NHPA Affiliation. Affiliate with the NHPA through the Sanctioned League program.

LEAGUE FORMAT

The basic concept of league play is that two teams play a match on a given day. Players of one team pitch against players from another team, and wins by individual pitchers count toward the team's win total. The ideal format, assuming sufficient facilities, is for one team to place its members on adjacent courts. The opposing team does the same, and the first round is pitched.

After the first round, one team's players rotate, moving over one court, and the second round of games is pitched. This is repeated until all possible rounds have been played. NHPA suggests you figure two to two and a half hours to pitch four fifty-shoe games.

Unfortunately, there are not always enough courts for the ideal format. Here are two ways to solve this problem.

Teams of Three on One Court, Singles. Each teammate pitches two forty-shoe games against each player from the other side. If only two players from a team are present (sometimes players sit out a match on a rotating basis), they each pitch three games. If only one teammate is present, he or she pitches all six games. Some leagues, trying to encourage attendance and discourage a team from fielding only its best player, will penalize a team if a single player pitches more than three games.

Teams of Three on One Court, Doubles. This follows the same format as teams of three on one court singles, except that partnerships are changed after one or two games so that everyone pitches the same number of games and a team will not keep its top two pitchers together.

The following scoring methods can be used for this format:

1. Twenty-shoe doubles. Each player pitches twenty shoes.
2. Fifty-shoe doubles. One player pitches twenty-four shoes, the other twenty-six shoes. In the second game, the first player pitches twenty-six shoes, the other twenty-four. Each game counts as a win, but a player's averages, scores, and handicaps are based on fifty shoes. Each player's handicap in the game is half his fifty-shoe handicap.
3. Fifty-point games, no handicaps used.

There are disadvantages to having more than one extra teammate per court. Players forced to sit out matches may cool off or lose interest. If this is a problem, consider these alternatives:

1. Separate into two divisions, each division pitching on a different day, or at different times on the same day. Plan a playoff between divisional champions to determine an overall champion.
2. Form two or more leagues, each of which can establish its own method of play.

Leagues can also be built around singles, doubles, or class (tournament-type) play. The following formats are some examples.

Singles on Ten Courts (Twenty Players). Half the players stay on one court all evening.

The other half move over one court after each game. Play four fifty-shoe games, count-all scoring, 100 percent handicap. A statistician keeps track of who has played whom and schedules court assignments accordingly. If there are more than twenty or an odd number of players, some players will draw a bye for one game. At the end of four rounds, all those who had byes will pitch to complete their four games. This format has flexibility in that players need not pitch every week.

Singles or Doubles on Ten Courts (Forty Players). Two games are played simultaneously on the same court. Sometimes called "walking doubles," in this format all four players pitch their shoes before they move to the other end of the court. It should be decided before the game which end pitches first.

Class Play. The members are classed, as in tournaments, by count-all ringer average or by a qualifying score. All competition is within the various classes. The classes may remain unchanged throughout the season or be changed periodically. This system works best for clubs with a large number of pitchers.

High-Low Doubles. Players are paired and teams are balanced by putting the highest average with the lowest, second high with second low, and so forth. At least one league that uses this system plays twenty-five-point games and bases handicaps on the standings. When a first-place team plays a fourth-place team, the fourth-place team receives four points. It's not very scientific, but it improves competition.

CONSIDERATIONS IN LEAGUE PLAY

Scheduling. When you first form your league, you may not know how many teams you will have. For maximum flexibility, schedule Team 1 against Team 2, and Team 3 against Team 4 the first week. If you started with four teams and two more sign on the second week, you can designate them 5 and 6 and switch to a six-team schedule. Take your schedule from a NHPA schedule card and play the last round first. Teams 5 and 6 can pitch a makeup match at some convenient time. (For a listing of schedules for matches between teams and individual pitchers, see the *Master Schedules* segment at the end of this chapter.)

Scorekeeping. Although not essential, it's desirable to keep pitching records for each player. Often those not pitching will keep score. If not, players can keep a clipboard and scoresheet with them as they pitch to record their own scores. The player pitching last in an inning records the score from the previous inning. Or, you can stash the clipboard at one end and record two scores at the same time. Club scores can be kept on a piece of painted plywood lined like a scoresheet; players record their scores in chalk, which are later transferred to a master sheet.

Handicaps. A handicap is a predetermined number of bonus points given to a player in addition to the actual, or "scratch," score pitched in a game. It may be applied in either of two ways: Both players have handicaps added to their scratch scores, with a weaker player having a higher handicap and a stronger player having a lower handicap, only the weaker player receives bonus points based on the difference between the two players' averages. Handicap systems have been devised for both applications.

If two pitchers who know their ringer percentage are playing in the backyard, the easiest handicap system, needing no charts, is simply to award the weaker player the number of points equal to the difference in ringer percentages. So, for example, if your ringer percentage is 30 percent and mine is 20 percent, I start a fifty-shoe game ahead 10–0. If we play a forty-shoe game, we adjust that figure by calculating 80 percent of our difference — .80 x 10 = 8. Thus, I begin the game ahead 8–0.

Theoretically, players of differing abilities will be made equal by using 100 percent handicaps, whereby you give the lower-average player bonus points equal to the difference in their respective averages. In practice, however, this can unfairly penalize a very good pitcher because he has less room for improvement in a particular game. Since the purpose of handicap play is to produce close competition, many leagues use either 80 percent or 90 percent of full handicap. A few leagues use 75 percent of handicap, but this almost guarantees that the stronger player or team will win.

Count-All Points Handicap System. The most popular method of play for handicapping is Count-All Points scoring. The customary rules are as follows:

1. Both players can score in the same inning, receiving credit for all points and ringers.
2. Games are of a fixed length, commonly forty or fifty shoes, although thirty- and even twenty-shoe games are popular.
3. Players alternate first pitch, regardless of who scored the most in the previous inning.
4. Games tied at the end of regulation play stand as ties; each player is credited with half a win.

Averages are determined by dividing a player's total points scored by number of games played. If you score, say, 210 points in seven games, your average is 30. Your handicap is the difference between your average (30) and the maximum number of points possible in a game (120 in a forty-shoe game). In this case, your handicap is 90 (120–30).

The following charts show 100, 90, and 80 percent handicaps for twenty, thirty, forty, and fifty-shoe games. Consider this example as you peruse the chart: I'm pitching a forty-shoe game against Walter Ray Williams. His point average for forty shoes is a robust 110, mine is 96. Using an 80 percent handicap system, I will begin the game with 19 points to his 8. Alternatively, we could start 11–0.

20 SHOE HANDICAP CHART

Point Avg.	Handicap 100%	90%	80%	Point Avg.	Handicap 100%	90%	80%	Point Avg.	Handicap 100%	90%	80%
60	0	0	0	40	20	18	16	20	40	36	32
59	1	1	1	39	21	19	17	19	41	37	33
58	2	2	2	38	22	20	13	18	42	38	34
57	3	3	3	37	23	21	18	17	43	39	34
56	4	4	3	36	24	22	19	16	44	40	35
55	5	5	4	35	25	23	20	15	45	41	36
54	6	6	5	34	26	23	21	14	45	41	37
53	7	6	6	33	27	24	22	13	47	42	38
52	8	7	6	32	28	25	22	12	48	43	38
51	9	8	7	31	29	26	23	11	49	44	39
50	10	9	8	30	30	27	24	10	50	45	40
49	11	10	9	29	31	28	25	9	51	46	41
48	12	11	10	28	32	29	26	8	52	47	42
47	13	12	10	27	33	30	26	8	52	47	42
46	14	13	11	26	34	31	27	6	54	49	43
45	15	14	12	25	36	32	28	5	55	50	44
44	16	14	13	24	36	32	24	4	56	50	45
43	17	15	14	23	37	33	30	3	57	51	46
42	18	16	14	22	38	34	30	2	58	52	46
41	19	17	15	21	39	35	31	1	59	53	47

30 SHOE HANDICAP CHART

Point Avg.	100%	90%	80%	Point Avg.	100%	90%	80%	Point Avg.	100%	90%	80%
90	0	0	0	60	30	27	24	30	60	54	48
89	1	1	1	59	31	28	25	29	61	55	49
88	2	2	2	58	32	29	26	38	62	56	50
87	3	3	2	57	33	30	26	27	63	57	50
86	4	4	3	56	32	31	27	26	64	58	51
85	5	5	4	55	35	32	28	25	65	59	52
84	6	5	5	54	36	32	29	24	66	59	53
83	7	6	6	53	37	33	30	23	67	60	54
82	8	7	6	52	38	33	30	22	68	61	54
81	9	8	7	51	39	34	31	21	69	62	56
80	10	9	8	50	40	36	32	20	70	63	56
79	11	10	9	49	41	36	33	19	71	64	57
78	12	11	10	48	42	37	34	18	72	65	58
77	13	12	10	47	43	36	34	17	73	66	58
76	14	13	11	46	44	39	35	16	74	67	59
75	15	14	12	45	45	40	36	15	75	68	60
74	16	14	13	44	46	40	37	14	76	68	61
73	17	15	14	43	47	41	38	13	77	69	62
72	18	16	14	42	48	42	38	12	78	70	62
71	19	17	15	41	49	43	39	11	79	71	63
70	20	18	16	40	50	44	40	10	80	72	64
69	21	19	17	39	51	45	41	9	81	73	65
68	22	20	18	38	52	46	42	8	82	74	66
67	23	21	18	37	53	47	42	7	83	74	66
66	24	22	19	36	55	48	43	6	84	75	67
65	25	23	20	35	55	49	44	5	85	76	68
64	26	23	21	34	56	49	45	4	86	76	69
63	27	24	22	33	57	50	46	3	87	77	70
62	28	25	22	32	58	50	46	2	88	78	70
61	29	26	23	31	59	51	47	1	89	79	71

40 SHOE HANDICAP CHART

Point Avg.	Handicap 100%	90%	80%	Point Avg.	Handicap 100%	90%	80%	Point Avg.	Handicap 100%	90%	80%
120	0	0	0	80	40	36	32	40	80	72	64
119	1	1	1	79	41	37	33	39	81	73	65
118	2	2	2	78	42	38	34	38	82	74	66
117	3	3	2	77	43	39	34	37	83	75	66
116	4	4	3	76	44	40	35	36	84	76	67
115	5	5	4	75	45	41	36	35	85	77	68
114	6	5	5	74	46	41	37	34	86	77	69
113	7	6	6	73	47	42	38	33	87	78	70
112	8	7	6	72	48	43	38	32	88	79	70
111	9	8	7	71	49	44	39	31	89	80	71
110	10	9	8	70	50	45	40	30	90	81	72
109	11	10	9	69	51	46	41	29	91	82	73
108	12	11	10	68	52	47	42	28	92	83	74
107	13	12	10	67	53	48	42	27	93	84	74
106	14	13	11	66	54	49	43	26	94	85	75
105	15	14	12	65	55	50	44	25	95	86	76
104	16	14	13	64	56	50	45	24	96	86	77
103	17	15	14	63	57	51	46	23	97	87	78
102	18	16	14	62	58	52	46	22	98	88	78
101	91	17	15	61	59	53	47	21	99	89	79
100	20	18	16	60	60	54	48	20	100	90	80
99	21	19	17	59	61	55	49	19	101	91	81
98	22	20	18	58	62	56	50	18	102	92	82
97	23	21	18	57	63	57	50	17	103	93	82
96	24	22	19	56	64	58	51	16	104	94	83
95	25	23	20	55	65	59	52	15	105	95	84
94	26	23	21	54	66	59	53	14	106	95	85
93	27	24	22	53	67	60	54	13	107	96	86
92	28	25	22	52	68	61	54	12	108	97	86
91	29	26	23	51	69	62	55	11	109	98	87
90	30	27	24	50	70	63	56	10	110	99	88
89	31	28	25	49	71	64	57	9	111	100	89
88	32	29	26	48	72	65	58	8	112	101	90
87	33	30	26	47	73	66	58	7	113	102	90
86	34	31	27	46	74	67	59	6	114	103	91
85	35	32	28	45	75	68	60	5	115	104	92
84	36	32	29	44	76	68	61	4	116	104	93
83	37	33	30	43	77	69	62	3	117	105	94
82	38	34	30	42	78	70	62	2	118	106	94
81	39	35	31	41	79	71	63	1	119	107	95

50 SHOE HANDICAP CHART

Point Avg.	Handicap 100%	90%	80%	Point Avg.	Handicap 100%	90%	80%	Point Avg.	Handicap 100%	90%	80%
150	0	0	0	99	51	46	41	49	101	91	81
149	1	1	1	98	52	47	42	48	102	92	82
148	2	2	2	97	53	48	42	47	103	93	82
147	3	3	2	96	54	49	43	46	104	94	83
146	4	4	3	95	55	50	44	45	105	95	84
145	5	5	4	94	56	50	45	44	106	95	85
144	6	5	5	93	57	51	46	43	107	96	86
143	7	6	6	92	58	52	46	42	108	97	86
142	8	7	6	91	59	53	47	41	109	98	87
141	9	8	7	90	60	54	48	40	110	99	88
140	10	9	8	89	61	55	49	39	111	100	89
139	11	10	9	88	62	56	50	38	112	101	90
138	12	11	10	87	63	57	50	37	113	102	90
137	13	12	10	86	64	58	51	36	114	103	91
136	14	13	11	85	65	59	52	35	115	104	92
135	15	14	12	84	66	59	53	34	116	104	93
134	16	14	13	83	67	60	54	33	117	105	94
133	17	15	14	82	68	61	54	32	118	106	94
132	18	16	14	81	69	62	55	31	119	107	95
131	19	17	15	80	70	63	56	30	120	108	96
130	29	18	16	79	71	64	57	29	121	109	97
129	21	19	17	78	72	65	58	28	122	110	98
128	22	20	18	77	73	66	58	27	123	111	98
127	23	21	18	76	64	67	59	26	124	112	99
126	24	22	19	75	75	68	60	25	125	113	100
125	25	23	20	74	76	68	61	24	126	113	101
124	26	23	21	73	77	69	62	23	127	114	102
123	27	24	22	72	78	70	62	22	128	115	102
122	28	25	22	71	79	71	63	21	129	116	103
121	29	26	23	70	80	72	64	20	130	117	104
120	30	27	24	69	81	73	65	19	131	118	105
119	31	28	25	68	82	74	66	18	132	119	106
118	32	29	26	67	83	75	66	17	133	120	106
117	33	30	26	66	84	76	67	16	134	121	107
116	34	31	27	65	85	77	68	15	135	122	108
115	35	32	28	64	86	77	69	14	136	122	109
114	36	32	29	63	87	78	70	13	137	123	110
113	37	33	30	62	88	79	70	12	138	124	110
112	38	34	30	61	89	80	71	11	139	125	111
111	39	35	31	60	90	81	72	10	140	126	112
110	40	36	32	59	91	82	73	9	141	127	113
109	41	37	33	58	92	83	74	8	142	128	114
108	42	38	34	57	93	84	74	7	143	129	114
107	43	39	34	56	94	85	75	6	144	130	115
106	44	40	35	55	95	86	76	5	145	131	116
105	45	41	36	54	96	86	77	4	146	131	117
104	46	41	37	53	97	87	78	3	147	132	118
103	47	42	38	52	98	88	78	2	148	133	118
102	48	43	38	51	99	89	79	1	149	134	119
101	49	44	39	50	100	90	80				
100	50	45	40								

Cancellation Scoring Handicap System

Shoe-Limit Games. This system converts a player's ringer percentage into points. A factor, or multiplier, is determined based on the number of shoes and the percentage of handicap, as shown in the following table.

Factors used to adjust players' ringer percentages for shoe-limit games, cancellation scoring:

		PERCENTAGE OF HANDICAP		
		100%	90%	80%
Number	50	1.5	1.35	1.2
of shoes	40	1.2	1.08	.96
in game	30	.90	.81	.72
or	6	.18	.162	.144
Overtime	4	.12	.108	.096

For example, if you use a 90 percent handicap and play forty-shoe games, the multiplier is 1.08.

So if Player "A" has a 47 percent ringer average, her adjusted average is 47 x 1.08 = 51. Player "B," who averages 30 percent, has an adjusted average of 30 x 1.08 = 32. The difference is 19, so Player "B" starts the game leading 19–0.

All the rules of cancellation scoring apply to this system, except that players should alternate first pitch, regardless of who scored the previous inning.

Point-Limit Games. This system, used infrequently, is usually played to fifty points. The lower-average player receives bonus points in certain innings, based on the difference between the two players' ringer percentages. But this is much more complicated than the scoring in shoe-limit games. Score sheets must be prepared in advance or scorekeepers given a chart to help them calculate handicaps. The best advice is to stay with shoe-limit games.

PRESIDENTIAL FITNESS AWARD

In response to a disturbing decline in physical fitness among the young, the Presidential Sports Award program was developed by the President's Council on Physical Fitness and Sports in 1972.

In cooperation with national sports organizations and associations, it seeks to motivate Americans to become more physically active. It emphasizes regular exercise rather than outstanding performance.

To be eligible for this award you must be at least ten years old and be willing to accept the challenge of personal fitness. You can achieve this in one or more of fifty-eight sports, including horseshoe pitching. You can earn awards in multiple categories.

To earn the award, first select the sport or activity level. Then keep a record of your participation in a fitness log. When you have fulfilled the qualifying standards, send the completed and signed fitness log, along with $6 per award ($8 in Canada, $10 for all other countries) to: Presidential Sports Award, P.O. Box 68207, Indianapolis, IN 46268.

In six weeks or less you will receive a certificate of achievement, a blazer patch, a sports bag identification tag, and a "shoe pocket" to hold your valuables while you work out.

The fitness requirements cannot be completed in less than twenty-five separate workouts. A single workout might be to bicycle 12 miles using five or more gears, swim $3/4$ of a mile, or pitch horseshoes for two hours.

To qualify for the award for horseshoe pitching, you must pitch horseshoes a minimum of fifty hours with no more than two hours per day credited to the total. Sanctioned league or tournament games may be used; 100 sanctioned games required. If a combination of practice time and official games is used, credit a half hour for each sanctioned game. More than two hours per day can be credited if playing in a sanctioned tournament.

NHPA REGIONAL DIRECTORS

Following is a list of all NHPA regional directors by state. If you want out-of-area tournament information, the NHPA encourages you to contact the appropriate regional director.

If you need multiple-state information, write to the NHPA Fifth vice president, who oversees the regional directors. For information on the NHPA in Canada, contact Jack Adams, 35 O'Neil Crescent, Saskatoon, SK, Canada, S7N 1W7, 306-373-5184.

Tournament Travel Contacts

ALABAMA
  Bill Calhoun, 1307 Clearmont St., Opelika, AL 36801, 334-745-2356

ALASKA
  Norman S. Rousey, Box 140, Palmer, AK 99645, 907-745-3618

ARIZONA
  Wayne Minnick, 116 S. Virginia, Prescott, AZ 86303, 602-571-1779

ARKANSAS
  Jerry Kahle, 75 Table Rock Drive #H1, Eureka Springs, AR 72632, 501-253-6879

CALIFORNIA
Northern
  Gail Sluys, 1721 San Ramon Way, Santa Rosa, CA 95409, 707-538-3128

Southern
  Dave Garbani, 317 E. Wilson Ave., Ridgecrest, CA 93555, 619-375-6376

COLORADO
  Keith Thompson, PO Box 295, Strasburg, CO 80136, 303-622-4451

CONNECTICUT
  George St. Pierre, 26 Beacon St., Unit 38B, Burlington, MA 01803, 617-273-4007

DELAWARE
  Ray Matlock, 202 Wellesley Ct., Walkersville, MD 21793, 301-846-3483

FLORIDA
  Richard Senger, 1190 12th St., Box 335, Eagle Lake, FL 33839, 813-294-8612

GEORGIA
  Al Sandham, 3958 Cotswold Drive, Lilburn, GA 30247, 404-921-5322

HAWAII
  John McCormack, 91-941 Kalapu Street, Ewa Beach, HI 96706, 808-689-8033

IDAHO
  Rich Rebman, Rt. 5, Box 5257, Herminston, OR 97838, 503-567-8560

IOWA
  Bob C. Walters, 1401 Edgington, Eldora, IA 50627, 515-858-3861

INDIANA
  Jim Shilling, 5044A CR 64, Clawson, MI 48017, 810-435-5259

KANSAS
  Duane Goodrich, 1244 SW 32nd, Topeka, KS 66611, 913-266-4745

KENTUCKY
  Omar Blacketer, 7912 3rd St., Louisville, KY 40214, 502-363-4657

LOUISIANA
  Ron Latiolais, 12102 Turry Road, Gonzales, LA 70737, 504-647-4992

MAINE
George St. Pierre, 26 Beacon St., Unit 38B, Burlington, MA 01803, 617-273-4007

MARYLAND
Ray Matlock, 202 Wellesley Ct., Walkersville, MD 21793, 301-846-3483

MICHIGAN
Steve Summerlin, 545 S. Marias, Clawson, MI 48017, 810-435-5259

MINNESOTA
Len Lipovsky, 14741 Guthrie Ave., Apple Valley, MN 55124, 612-953-0888

MASSACHUSETTS
George St. Pierre, 26 Beacon St., Unit 38B, Burlington, MA 01803, 617-273-4007

MISSISSIPPI
Bill Calhoun, 1307 Clearmont St., Opelika, AL 36801, 334-745-2356

MISSOURI
Elwyn Cooper, 6920 N.W. 78th St., Kansas City, MO 64152, 816-741-0043

MONTANA
Rich Paul, 2223 3rd Ave. N., Great Falls, MT 59403, 406-452-7246

NORTH CAROLINA
Paul Stewart, 1043 Old Mountain Rd., Statesville, NC 28677, 704-528-5081

NORTH DAKOTA
Clint Bryson, 901 Custer St., Belle Fourche, SD 57717, 605-892-2195

NEVADA
Don Weaver, 2206 Sunnyslope Ave., Las Vegas, NV 89119, 702-736-7348

NEW HAMPSHIRE
George St. Pierre, 26 Beacon St., Unit 38B, Burlington, MA 01803, 617-273-4007

NEW JERSEY
Phil Zozzaro, 176 Main St., Apt. D, Little Falls, NJ 07424, 201-256-8996

NEW MEXICO
Hal Mineer, PO Box 462, Sandia Park, NM 87047, 505-281-9794

NEW YORK
Lance Twyman, 6320 CR 27, Canton, NY 13617, 315-386-2404

OHIO
Earl VanSant, 244 Deer Drive, Charden, OH 44024, 216-285-2552

OKLAHOMA
Chuck Arnold, 10024 Millspaugh Way, Yukon, OK 73099, 405-324-7161

OREGON
Rick Rebman, Rt. 4, Box 5257, Herminston, OR 97838, 503-567-8560

PENNSYLVANIA

Frank Kallay, 25 Tanager Drive, McKees Rocks, PA 15136, 412-33

RHODE ISLAND

George St. Pierre, 26 Beacon St., Unit 38B, Burlington, MA 01803, 617-273-4007

SOUTH CAROLINA

Ron Taylor, 116 Knox St., Clover, SC 29710, 803-222-3990

SOUTH DAKOTA

Clint Bryson, 901 Custer St., Belle Fourche, SD 57717, 605-892-2195

TENNESSEE

Dexter Stallings, 731 Reed Drive, Powell, TN 37849, 615-947-7865

TEXAS

Hazel McCall, 4000 Huaco Lane, Waco, TX 76710, 817-756-0771

UTAH

Bud Schardine, 354 Brookside Drive, Springville, UT 84663, 801-489-6351

VERMONT

George St. Pierre, 26 Beacon St., Unit 38B, Burlington, MA 01803, 617-273-4007

VIRGINIA

Earl Waggy, 504 W. Bank St., Bridgewater, VA 22812, 703-828-3816

WASHINGTON

Rick Rebman, Rt. 5, Box 5257, Herminston, OR 97838, 503-567-8560

WEST VIRGINIA

Herb Murray, 1303 Clyde St., Parkersburg, WV 26101, 304-428-5646

WISCONSIN

Jim Haupt, 5075 N. Elkhart Ave., Milwaukee, WI 53217, 414-964-2735

WYOMING

Harold Koch, 801 Metz Road, Gillette, WY 82718, 307-682-8688

Master Schedules

Schedules for matches between two teams of four, five, six and eight players each.

FOUR PLAYERS

	Court			
Round	1	2	3	4
1	1-5	3-8	2-6	4-7
2	4-8	2-5	3-7	1-6
3	2-7	4-6	1-8	3-5
4	3-6	1-7	4-5	2-8

FIVE PLAYERS

	Court				
Round	1	2	3	4	5
1	4-6	3-7	5-9	2-8	1-10
2	3-8	2-10	4-7	1-9	5-6
3	2-9	1-6	3-10	5-7	4-8
4	1-7	5-8	2-6	4-10	3-9
5	5-10	4-9	1-8	3-6	2-7

SIX PLAYERS

	Court					
	1	**2**	**3**	**4**	**5**	**6**
1	5-10	6-9	3-8	4-7	1-12	2-11
2	2-9	1-10	6-7	5-8	4-11	3-12
3	3-11	4-12	2-10	1-9	5-7	6-8
4	4-8	3-7	1-11	2-12	6-10	5-9
5	1-7	2-8	5-12	6-11	3-9	4-10
6	6-12	5-11	4-9	3 10	1-8	2-7

(Round)

EIGHT PLAYERS

	Court							
	1	**2**	**3**	**4**	**5**	**6**	**7**	**8**
1	2-12	3-9	4-10	1-11	6-16	7-13	8-14	5-15
2	1-9	2-10	3-11	4-12	5-13	6-14	7-15	8-16
3	7-11	8-12	5-9	6-10	3-15	4-16	1-13	2-14
4	8-10	5-11	6-12	7-9	4-14	1-15	2-16	3-13
5	6-13	7-14	8-15	5-16	2-9	3-10	4-11	1-12
6	3-16	4-13	1-14	2-15	7-12	8-9	5-10	6-11
7	4-15	1-16	2-13	3-14	8-11	5-12	6-9	7-10
8	5-14	6-15	7-16	8-13	1-10	2-11	3-12	4-9

(Round)

Round Robin Master Schedules

FOUR-PERSON ROUND ROBIN

	Court 1	Court 2
Round 1	1-4	2-3
2	2-4	1-3
3	1-2	3-4

SIX-PERSON ROUND ROBIN

	Court 1	Court 2	Court 3
Round 1	2-5	3-6	1-4
2	4-6	1-5	2-3
3	1-3	2-6	4-5
4	2-4	3-5	1-6
5	5-6	1-2	3-4

EIGHT-PERSON ROUND ROBIN

	Court 1	Court 2	Court 3	Court 4
Round 1	3-7	4-8	1-5	2-6
2	2-8	1-3	4-6	5-7
3	1-7	2-4	3-5	6-8
4	3-6	5-8	2-7	1-4
5	4-5	6-7	1-8	2-3
6	3-8	2-5	4-7	1-6
7	1-2	3-4	5-6	7-8

TEN-PERSON ROUND ROBIN

		Court			
Round	**1**	**2**	**3**	**4**	**5**
1	4-6	3-7	5-9	2-8	1-10
2	3-8	2-10	4-7	1-5	6-9
3	2-5	1-6	3-10	7-9	4-8
4	1-7	8-9	2-6	4-10	3-5
5	2-9	4-5	1-3	6-8	7-10
6	5-7	1-9	8-10	2-4	3-6
7	6-10	5-8	1-4	3-9	2-7
8	4-9	6-7	2-3	5-10	1-8
9	1-2	3-4	5-6	7-8	9-10

TWELVE-PERSON ROUND ROBIN

		Court				
Round	**1**	**2**	**3**	**4**	**5**	**6**
1	4-7	1-12	2-11	3-8	6-9	5-10
2	6-11	3-9	4-10	5-12	2-8	1-7
3	5-8	4-11	3-12	6-7	1-10	2-9
4	1-9	5-7	6-8	2-10	4-12	3-11
5	2-12	6-10	5-9	1-11	3-7	4-8
6	3-10	1-8	2-7	4-9	5-11	6-12
7	8-11	9-12	1-4	7-10	3-6	2-5
8	3-5	8-10	7-12	1-6	2-4	9-11
9	7-9	2-6	10-11	4-5	8-12	1-3
10	10-12	7-11	2-3	8-9	1-5	4-6
11	1-2	3-4	5-6	11-12	9-10	7-8

14-PERSON ROUND ROBIN

	Court 1	2	3	4	5	6	7
1	2-9	6-12	1-13	8-10	3-11	4-7	5-14
2	3-10	2-14	4-5	7-11	6-9	1-12	8-13
3	4-12	1-9	8-14	6-13	5-7	2-3	10-11
4	2-13	4-11	6-10	9-12	1-8	7-14	3-5
5	6-11	5-10	7-9	1-14	4-13	3-12	2-8
6	9-14	7-13	5-11	2-12	3-8	1-10	4-6
7	3-13	4-14	6-8	1-11	2-10	5-9	7-12
8	5-12	2-7	3-14	4-9	1-6	8-11	10-13
9	7-10	11-13	9-8	3-6	12-14	2-5	1-4
10	6-14	8-12	2-11	5-13	1-7	4-10	3-9
11	4-8	1-5	3-7	10-12	11-14	9-13	2-6
12	9-11	10-14	12-13	2-4	5-8	6-7	1-3
13	1-2	3-4	5-6	7-8	9-10	11-12	13-14

(Rows labeled under "Round")

16-PERSON ROUND ROBIN

	Court 1	2	3	4	5	6	7	8
1	1-9	2-10	3-11	4-12	5-13	6-14	7-15	8-16
2	2-12	3-9	4-10	1-11	6-16	7-13	8-14	5-15
3	7-11	8-12	5-9	6-10	3-15	4-16	1-13	2-14
4	8-10	5-11	6-12	7-9	4-14	1-15	2-16	3-13
5	6-13	7-14	8-15	5-16	2-9	3-10	4-11	1-12
6	3-16	4-13	1-14	2-15	7-12	8-9	5-10	6-11
7	4-15	1-16	2-13	3-14	8-11	5-12	6-9	7-10
8	5-14	6-15	7-16	8-13	1-10	2-11	3-12	4-9
9	3-6	9-16	10-13	4-7	11-14	1-8	2-5	12-15
10	12-14	2-8	9-15	3-5	4-6	10-16	1-7	11-13
11	1-5	11-15	2-6	12-16	9-13	3-7	10-14	4-8
12	9-11	10-12	14-16	13-15	1-3	2-4	6-8	5-7
13	13-16	6-7	1-4	10-11	5-8	14-15	9-12	2-3
14	10-15	4-5	3-8	9-14	2-7	12-13	11-16	1-6
15	7-8	13-14	11-12	1-2	15-16	5-6	3-4	9-10

(Rows labeled under "Round")

18-PERSON ROUND ROBIN

Round	Court 1	2	3	4	5	6	7	8	9
1	2-9	1-17	10-12	4-8	3-18	6-14	5-7	13-15	11-16
2	8-13	9-12	3-15	7-10	2-6	11-17	14-16	1-18	4-5
3	6-18	2-16	8-17	1-15	9-11	5-13	4-10	12-14	3-7
4	4-16	15-17	2-12	3-5	10-13	7-18	6-9	8-11	1-14
5	7-15	6-11	5-9	4-17	8-16	3-12	1-13	2-14	10-18
6	5-17	8-10	14-18	2-7	1-12	4-15	3-11	6-13	9-16
7	3-14	4-18	1-11	6-8	5-15	2-10	16-17	7-9	12-13
8	1-10	3-13	6-7	11-18	4-14	5-16	2-15	12-17	8-9
9	16-18	4-11	10-17	14-15	2-13	1-9	7-12	5-8	3-6
10	7-17	8-15	9-14	2-5	1-16	12-18	3-10	4-6	11-13
11	3-9	2-18	1-8	13-16	10-15	6-17	5-12	11-14	4-7
12	6-15	3-16	5-18	14-17	4-12	10-11	9-13	1-7	2-8
13	4-13	7-14	12-16	8-18	3-17	9-15	2-11	5-10	1-6
14	10-14	1-5	2-17	4-9	7-11	3-8	6-16	13-18	12-15
15	8-12	13-17	11-15	6-10	9-18	7-16	1-4	2-3	5-14
16	5-11	6-12	7-13	1-3	8-14	2-4	15-18	9-17	10-16
17	1-2	9-10	3-4	11-12	5-6	13-14	7-8	15-16	17-18

20-PERSON ROUND ROBIN

Round	Court 1	2	3	4	5	6	7	8	9	10
1	1-20	2-19	3-18	4-17	5-16	6-15	7-14	8-13	9-12	10-11
2	4-15	5-14	6-13	7-12	9-10	18-20	8-11	3-16	2-17	1-19
3	8-9	4-13	5-12	2-15	16-20	7-10	17-19	6-11	1-18	3-14
4	14-20	16-18	4-11	5-10	7-8	3-12	2-13	1-17	15-19	6-9
5	13-19	12-20	15-17	14-18	3-10	2-11	1-16	6-7	4-9	5-8
6	5-6	1-15	10-20	3-8	2-9	14-16	13-17	12-18	11-19	4-7
7	11-17	10-18	1-14	2-7	4-5	8-20	9-19	13-15	3-6	12-16
8	10-16	7-19	2-5	1-13	8-18	9-17	12-14	3-4	11-15	6-20
9	11-13	2-3	8-16	9-15	1-12	5-19	4-20	6-18	10-14	7-17
10	2-20	9-13	7-15	10-12	6-16	1-11	3-19	5-17	4-18	8-14
11	8-12	6-14	9-11	20-19	7-13	3-17	1-10	4-16	5-15	2-18
12	18-19	7-11	6-12	8-10	3-15	5-13	4-14	1-9	2-16	17-20
13	7-9	20-15	3-13	16-19	17-18	4-12	6-10	2-14	1-8	5-11
14	3-11	6-8	14-19	5-9	4-10	15-18	2-12	20-13	16-17	1-7
15	1-6	3-9	5-7	4-8	14-17	2-10	11-20	15-16	12-19	13-18
16	14-15	12-17	2-8	9-20	11-18	4-6	3-7	10-19	13-16	1-5
17	10-17	8-19	1-4	2-6	13-14	3-5	12-15	9-18	7-20	11-16
18	2-4	12-13	7-18	1-3	6-19	8-17	9-16	5-20	11-14	10-15
19	8-15	7-16	10-13	11-12	1-2	9-14	5-18	4-19	6-17	3-20

24-PERSON ROUND ROBIN

Round	Court 1	Court 2	Court 3	Court 4	Court 5	Court 6	Court 7	Court 8	Court 9	Court 10	Court 11	Court 12
1	1-24	2-23	3-22	10-15	4-21	12-13	6-9	8-17	9-16	7-18	11-14	5-20
2	12-11	13-10	14-9	8-5	7-16	23-1	22-24	2-21	4-19	3-20	5-18	6-17
3	4-17	3-18	8-13	20-24	1-22	5-16	21-23	6-15	7-14	2-19	9-12	10-11
4	20-22	1-21	18-24	9-13	2-17	4-15	8-11	5-14	6-13	7-12	3-16	19-23
5	6-11	16-24	1-20	18-22	4-13	3-14	2-15	7-10	5-12	19-21	17-23	8-9
6	7-8	6-9	4-11	3-12	14-24	18-20	5-10	1-19	17-21	15-23	2-13	16-22
7	3-10	14-22	2-11	1-18	17-19	6-7	13-23	12-24	4-9	16-20	4-7	5-8
8	5-6	15-19	13-21	11-23	3-8	12-22	1-17	16-18	10-24	2-9	15-21	14-20
9	8-24	20-12	14-18	4-5	11-21	1-16	9-23	15-17	3-6	13-19	10-22	2-7
10	1-15	2-5	10-20	13-17	12-18	9-21	14-16	8-22	7-23	3-4	11-19	6-24
11	10-18	11-17	12-16	9-19	4-24	2-3	8-20	7-21	1-14	6-22	5-23	13-15
12	12-14	18-8	7-19	4-22	6-20	1-15	3-23	1-13	9-17	2-24	10-16	5-21
13	8-16	9-15	10-14	11-13	1-12	23-24	2-22	3-21	4-20	5-19	6-18	7-17
14	21-24	22-23	9-13	10-12	8-14	7-15	19-24	20-23	4-18	3-19	2-20	1-11
15	1-10	2-18	4-16	5-17	5-15	5-11	8-10	1-9	21-22	3-15	7-13	6-14
16	5-13	7-11	18-23	16-23	2-16	17-24	19-20	4-12	6-12	2-14	19-22	20-21
17	7-9	6-10	17-22	16-23	5-11	16-21	14-23	15-22	15-24	17-20	1-8	3-13
18	3-11	13-24	2-12	1-7	4-10	6-8	1-6	4-8	5-9	13-22	21-16	18-19
19	16-19	14-21	11-24	15-20	3-9	17-18	11-22	14-19	2-10	15-18	5-7	12-23
20	6-4	1-5	3-7	8-2	12-21	13-20	7-24	2-6	17-16	10-21	10-23	24-9
21	12-19	14-17	15-16	13-18	9-22	3-5	12-17	13-16	8-23	10-21	4-1	11-20
22	6-23	9-20	2-4	5-24	11-15	8-21	2-1	9-18	3-1	7-22	10-19	14-15
23	7-20	8-19	5-22	6-21	12-15	4-23	1-18	2-9	13-14	3-24	11-16	10-17

Round Robin Schedules for Uneven Numbers of Pitchers

FIVE PLAYERS ON TWO STAKES

	Court	
Round	1	2
1	2-5	1-4
2	1-5	2-3
3	1-3	4-5
4	2-4	3-5
5	1-2	3-4

SEVEN PLAYERS ON THREE STAKES

	Court		
Round	1	2	3
1	3-7	1-5	2-6
2	1-3	4-6	5-7
3	1-7	2-4	3-5
4	3-6	2-7	1-4
5	4-5	6-7	2-3
6	2-5	4-7	1-6
7	1-2	3-4	5-6

NINE PLAYERS ON FOUR STAKES

	Court			
	1	**2**	**3**	**4**
1	4-6	3-7	5-9	2-8
2	3-8	4-7	1-5	6-9
3	2-5	1-6	7-9	4-8
4	1-7	8-9	2-6	3-5
5	2-9	4-5	1-3	6-8
6	5-7	1-9	2-4	3-6
7	5-8	1-4	3-9	2-7
8	4-9	6-7	2-3	1-8
9	1-2	3-4	5-6	7-8

Round